GW00382613

MISSIONARIES
from
IRELAND
NOW WITH THE LORD

Compiled by

J.G. HUTCHINSON

OCTOBER 1988
Published by
GOSPEL TRACT PUBLICATIONS
411 Hillington Road, Glasgow G52 4BL, Scotland

ISBN 0 948417 38 2
Copyright © 1988
J.G. Hutchinson

Typeset, printed and bound by
GOSPEL TRACT PUBLICATIONS
411 Hillington Road, Glasgow G52 4BL, Scotland

My album is the savage breast,
Where darkness reigns and tempests wrest;
Without one ray of light.
To write the name of Jesus there
And point to worlds both bright and fair
And see the savage bow in prayer;
Is my supreme delight.

R. Moffat.

Contents

Preface

Ireland is a small island on the fringe of Western Europe with a population of approximately five million. Yet, it is a cause for wonder, at the contribution its people have made in almost every part of the world, in politics, commerce, and particularly in religious matters. From it many noble men and women have gone worldwide carrying the gospel message. It would be impossible for any human being to accurately assess all that has been accomplished for the glory of God and the blessing of men. This the "righteous Judge" will do in a coming day. I have endeavoured to do a little research and put together some facts regarding some of the men "who hazarded their lives"—"for My sake and the gospel's". It would be interesting and helpful to have full records of other godly, spiritual men and women; these records are in the hands of One who makes no mistakes.

More is written about some mentioned in this volume than about others; this is simply because it has been difficult to get information. These dear men did not publicise their work, project themselves or seek their own interests. Many were like the disciple who would wish to stay in the background and say, "The disciple whom Jesus loved".

May the reading of these pages increase our appreciation of those who have left home and friends and at the same time stir hearts to greater zeal in making known the gospel. Some whose labours we have mentioned, had they stayed at home would have succeeded in professional and business life, possibly amassing large amounts of money and enjoying comparative ease. As we view them now we ask, which is "the better part"? A prominent and wealthy

7

business man died in Canada; apart from a mention of the amount of his estate, all that was said in a local paper was, "He was a brother of the well-known missionary David Livingstone". Another writing about a devoted missionary said, "He had contemporaries; where are his successors?". May the Lord of the Harvest help young people with health, education and privilege to "look on the fields". "The harvest truly is plenteous, but the labourers are few".

I acknowledge with sincere thanks the help of many in giving me information and photographs. I would also thank Miss E. Glasgow BA who typed all the material; I appreciate her patience and help. Mr James Johnston BA has read and corrected the material, as well as making valuable suggestions; he also is due sincere thanks.

James G Hutchinson

July 1988

Foreword

It is a great honour and privilege to pay tribute to the memory of godly and dedicated servants of the Lord who have finished their course and are now in the presence of the Lord. Some were taken home after a comparatively short period of service while others were spared to serve the Lord for a long lifetime. It is a repetition of what happened in the early church. The Lord asked the two brothers James and John, "Are you able to drink of the cup that I shall drink of, and be baptized with the baptism that I am baptized with?" They replied, "We are able" (Matt. 20-22). It is very unlikely that the brothers understood the full meaning of our Lord's words. But as far as James was concerned, we find its fulfilment in Acts 12:1-2, "Now about that time Herod the king stretched forth his hands to vex certain of the church. And he killed James the brother of John with the sword." James had a very short time of service and then, martyrdom. This is the last time John is mentioned in the Acts. But we know that he had a long fruitful life, outliving all the other apostles and finally had his baptism of suffering under the persecuting Roman emperor Domitian.

Robert John Johnston sailed from Belfast with Mr H.B. Thompson in June 1889. As the ship left the quay, waving farewell, he pointed upward and said, "Heaven is as near to Africa as it is to Belfast." One month later, in the harbour at Benguela in Angola, the Lord called him home. His work was finished. Benjamin Cobbe, who had laboured in the Gospel with Mr Wm. Gilmore in Ireland, on landing in Africa said: "I have come to pay my debt." He joined Fred Stanley Arnot on his journey to Luanza in August 1894

9

and passed away on May 2nd 1896. He had paid his debt to
the needy in dark Africa with his life. These brethren, like
James the brother of John had been baptized with the
baptism of suffering in God's sovereign purpose.

On the other hand William Maitland of Chokweland,
John Ruddock of Honduras and many others, in spite of
danger, disease and incredible hardships, were spared for
more than 50 years, and the results of their labours remain
until the present day.

This book gives a record of the dedicated work of a
number of men of God who had their roots in Ireland. Of
necessity their life's history is sketchy and incomplete. But
the details are on high and will all come out in the morning.
"Then shall every man have praise of God" (1 Cor. 4:5).

We who remain, humbly render our honour, thanksgiving
and respect to their memory.

T. Ernest Wilson.

The Missionary

His Call, Character, Commendation, Commission and Compensation.

The servant of the Lord, the Messiah, our Lord Jesus Christ, is the main theme of Isaiah 40-66. There are seven lovely pictures of Him in these chapters. He is the Shepherd (ch.40:11); Servant (ch.42); Soldier (ch.49); Scholar (ch.50); Sufferer (ch.53); Saviour (ch.55); Sovereign Lord (ch.63). In chapter 42 He is God's sent Servant. There we have His call, character, commendation, commission and, in the last paragraph of chapter 53, His compensation as a result of His sacrificial sufferings. He is our great Pattern and Example for the servant of the Lord today. After His resurrection, in commissioning His disciples He said, "As my Father hath sent me, even so, send I you."

We sometimes make a distinction between an Evangelist and a Missionary; one confines his service to the home field and the other goes overseas and maybe has to learn one or several languages. But, after all, the work is one and the Scriptural principles connected with service are obligatory for both.

(1)   God's Call to Special Service.

It has been held and taught by some, that the only call one needs to serve the Lord is the Great Commission of Matthew 28:18-20. In one sense this is true. Every believer without distinction has the responsibility to be a witness for Christ in the sphere where God has placed him or her. But, on the other hand, the Bible makes it crystal clear that God in His sovereignty chooses and fits and sends certain

11

individuals to do a specific work. They are called by God. They are brought into the Sanctuary, the secret place of the Most High, and there God speaks to them through His Word. There are at least seven men in the Old Testament who were called by God. The details of that call are recorded. Each one is different, but the principle is the same. The names are: Abraham, Moses, Gideon, Elisha, Isaiah, Jeremiah and Ezekiel. The same rule is exemplified in the New Testament; we read of the call of Simon Peter, of Paul the Apostle and of Timothy the Evangelist. The person who leaves home and goes thousands of miles away into some mission field without a clear conviction of the call of God is to be pitied. This is the reason for many breakdowns and drop-outs.

(2)   The Character of the Missionary.

The moral behaviour of the prospective missionary must be beyond reproach. Living in isolation in a pagan environment, he will be exposed to all kinds of subtle temptations. The same, of course, is true in so-called civilised countries. What has been his attitude to the opposite sex in his home country? Paul advised Timothy: "Keep thyself pure" 1 Timothy 5:22. Has he had the discipline of earning his living honestly, of obeying orders and being punctual, and learning how to spend money wisely? These things are important. There is a danger in a tropical climate of becoming lethargic and lazy and not doing a full day's work.

In spiritual things, is he a careful diligent student of the Word of God, well-balanced, rightly dividing the Word of truth? One of the greatest needs among the assemblies, both at home and abroad, is men who can build and bind and beautify the people of God. He must be a man of prayer and faith. In this connection the qualifications of elders in 1 Tim.3 and Titus 1 are relevant and should be read and studied again and again.

(3)   The Missionary's Commendation.

The classic passage is Acts 13:1-4. Barnabas and Saul

(Paul) had been believers for a number of years. Since conversion both had been active in service for the Lord. Now they are named as among the leaders in the church at Antioch. But God had a special work for them to do. The Holy Spirit spoke, possibly through one of the elders: "Separate me Barnabas and Saul for the work unto which I have called them." Note: already they had been called by God. Now it is the responsibility of the local church to act. "And when they had fasted and prayed, and laid their hands upon them, they sent them away (they let them go—J.N.D.). So they being sent forth by the Holy Spirit departed unto Seleucia." First, there is God's call, then the voice of the Holy Spirit, followed by deep exercise and prayer on the part of the local church. The laying on of their hands indicates their fellowship and identification with the missionaries; and, finally, it is the Holy Spirit who sends them forth.

In our day, the laying on of hands is usually symbolized by the local assembly writing a letter of commendation signed by the elders indicating their fellowship and confidence in the person going forth into the work. This is a solemn responsibility, not to be taken lightly. The signers of the letter must be sure that the prospective missionary has been called by God, and is fitted both spiritually, morally, mentally and emotionally for the work. A person who cannot work harmoniously with his brethren at home, or is short-tempered or unwilling to take advice, could be a menace on the mission field.

Many foreign governments today require a guarantee, that, if, for any reason, the missionary has to be repatriated, it is the commending assembly that is ultimately financially responsible. Without this guarantee a visa to enter and remain in the country is often refused. All of this places a heavy weight of responsibility on those who sign a letter of commendation. Little wonder the assembly at Antioch fasted and prayed before they laid their hands on Barnabas and Saul and "let them go!"

(4)   The Missionary's Commission.

The Great Commission of the Risen Christ to His

disciples in Matthew's Gospel ch.28:18-20 is fivefold:

(1) All authority is given unto me in heaven and in earth.

(2) Go ye, therefore, and make disciples of all nations (R.V.)

(3) Baptizing them into the name of the Father and of the Son and of the Holy Ghost.

(4) Teaching them to observe all things whatsoever I commanded you.

(5) And lo, I am with you alway, even unto the consummation of the age (R.V. marg.).

There are four imperatives: Go. Make disciples: Baptize. Teach. The commands are enclosed in two promises: The assurance of His omnipotent power and authority, and the promise of His presence with them to the end of the age.

The Acts of the Apostles gives a graphic account of the carrying out of this commission. Its main theme is the preaching of the Gospel and the planting of local assemblies. Starting in Jerusalem, the religious capital of the world, inside a single generation the Gospel had spread to the political capital, the city of Rome. In less than 20 years churches had been established at strategic centres in four of the provinces of the Roman empire. This is the pattern for the missionary today. Conditions have changed but the basic plan and principles are the same and have been recorded as our example to follow. First and foremost the objective of all missionary work must be the preaching of the Gospel and the planting of New Testament assemblies. Then the converts must be taught the great doctrines of Holy Scripture. This is not a short-term project; it will occupy a lifetime in carrying it out. In a pioneer field there will be many problems and difficulties. Sometimes a language or languages have to be learned and committed to writing. After that, the Word of God must be translated into the vernacular and the Bible printed, usually by a Bible Society overseas. Then a school must be organized to teach the people how to read. The present writer spent 40 years under a Portuguese government in Angola. We were required by law to do educational work in the Portuguese language among Africans, who spoke only their native Bantu dialects. The law demanded and was strictly enforced, that we offer medical assistance to the people when they were sick or injured. This meant that every missionary centre was obliged to have either a dispensary or a hospital with competent and qualified personnel. While basically our main object was to preach the Gospel and plant assemblies according to the New Testament pattern, these by-products of practical Christianity were greatly blessed in the salvation of souls and the upbuilding of the work.

At this point, the writer would like to pay tribute to the many godly, dedicated women commended by the assemblies in the homeland, who have given a lifetime of service to this work. Both our Lord Himself and Dr. Luke in his Gospel were especially appreciative of the worship and work of the women who followed and ministered unto Him. Luke 8:2-3. "She hath done what she could" Mark 14:8; John 12:1-8. In Africa their work has been principally among women and children, teaching school, in medical work, the treatment and care of lepers, translation, etc, etc. At Capango, among the Umbundu speaking people, where we spent the last 20 years of our service in Angola, there are the graves of five missionaries, who have given their lives for the Lord in His work. One is a man, the other four are women. I was present at the burial of two of them. Some served for a comparatively short time, but others for more than 50 years. The Lord of the Harvest will surely recognize and reward in that day.

(5)   The Missionary's Recompense.

It has often been said that the highest honour that could be conferred on any Christian is to be chosen by God to be an ambassador for Christ in a pioneer field in a foreign land. On the one hand it could involve isolation, exposure to strange diseases, persecution, depression, danger and even death. But, on the other hand, it has its compensations. On one occasion, Simon Peter said to the Lord: "Lo, we have left all, and have followed thee." The Lord replied: "Verily I say unto you, There is no man that hath left house, or brethren, or sisters, or father, or mother, or wife, or children, or lands, for my sake, and the gospel's; but he shall receive an hundredfold now in this time, houses and brethren, and sisters, and mothers, and children, and lands, with persecutions; and in the age to come eternal life" Mark 10:28-30. Many a veteran missionary can testify that this promise has been literally fulfilled, in their lifetime of service. And then there is the *Bema*, the judgment seat of Christ. Paul could say of his dear friends, brought to Christ through his labours at Thessalonica: "For what is our hope, or joy, or crown of rejoicing? Are not even ye in the presence of our Lord Jesus Christ at His coming? For ye are our glory and joy" 1 Thess. 2:19-20. A glad reunion of the missionary and his children in the Lord.

But the greatest compensation of all will be to hear the commendation of the Lord of the Harvest, our Lord Jesus Christ: "Well done, good and faithful servant, enter thou into the joy of thy Lord."

MR HERBERT BEATTIE

1921-1978

Mr Beattie was a native of Belfast and was saved when he was eleven years old. Mr Peter Major, having returned from missionary work in the Dominican Republic, was conducting special meetings in Ballynure Street Gospel Hall. Bertie, along with quite a number of others, including one who was later to become his wife, Miss Margaret McAlistar, came to know the Saviour. He was baptised and received into the assembly, which later became known as Oldpark Gospel Hall, and was active in christian work. He accepted responsibility as superintendent of the Sunday school and saw it grow to three hundred members. He also shared in the village work—a work that God blessed and used as a training ground for a number who have turned out to be useful evangelists and missionaries.

He was employed in Belfast with a printing firm and trained as a compositor. In 1946, he was commended to the work of the Lord in France. Earlier he had exercise of heart regarding China, but later was convinced he should serve the Lord in Europe. He did language study in L'Alliance Francaise in Paris. Until 1961, he and his wife served from their home in France, preaching the gospel and distributing gospel literature amongst a very needy, but indifferent pleasure-loving people. Along with Mr G. Jones and Mr T. McAdams, he conducted tent meetings between 1948 and 1951. These resulted in much blessing and in 1954 a permanent building was acquired, which was situated near to Gobelins Metro station. This provided the assembly

with a good hall and a flat above it, suitable for a full-time worker.

The Gobelins assembly had an outreach work at Conflans Sainte Honorine, where Brian Tatford, James Yorgey and some young men had fruitful meetings. In 1955, an assembly was formed and Bertie and his wife moved there with a view to consolidating the work. For some time the assembly met in the basement of a garage, but subsequently a fine hall was built on the outskirts of the city on land provided by the local believers. Bertie did some pioneer work in St Etienne, and later resided for a period at Le Chambon-sur-Lignon, seeking to care for the assembly and engage in camp activities.

In view of the education of their family, they decided to return to the UK, making their home in Bury St Edmunds. It was a short journey from there to France and for the remaining years of his life, Bertie crossed from England to France, engaging in a variety of christian work in France, Italy, and Belgium, preaching the gospel, speaking at conferences and leading camp work.

His personality was pleasant and his winning way endeared him to people of all age groups. His spirit was bright and buoyant, thus people were cheered and uplifted by his company. Allied with all this was a deep spirituality, demonstrated in his public prayers and ministry of the Word, either to the perishing in the gospel, or to the believers in teaching the Scriptures. His visitation and counsel were also appreciated.

On 21st April, 1978 he was stricken with a severe heart attack, and he passed away very suddenly. He had given thirty-two years of devoted service to the Lord and He will fully and suitably reward, Heb. 6:10. His brethren in Bury said, "His Christ-like life was an example to all of us; his passing is greatly mourned by many".

MR JAMES CASTLES
1874-1943

Mr Castles was born on 22nd September, 1874 in the Lurgan distict, and for some years was well-known as the local postman. He was saved in early life and associated with the Ardmore assembly, which at that time was small and met in the home of a Mr Emerson. Mr Castles was active in gospel work, speaking personally to the local people in the course of his daily duties, and preaching in the evening in the open-air, at house meetings and wherever the people gathered. When his exercise about the work of the gospel matured and he approached his brethren regarding going to South America, they whole-heartedly commended him to the work in 1904.

He married Miss Kathleen McCann who came from Belfast, and had been commended to the work by Ormeau Road Assembly, Belfast in 1910. They were married in Tucuman in Argentina, and soon after made their home in Salta, where their two sons, James and Stuart, were born. James died when a very small child. After the birth of their daughter they returned to Belfast on furlough in 1920.

He had laboured in Montevideo in Uruguay from 1909-1911, going from there to Salta, and after returning to South America, a short time was spent again in Montevideo; then he moved to Sandose near Fray Bentos, and later to San Jose, where the work prospered and an assembly was formed, which has grown quite considerably over the years.

At Mendoza, he with Mr A. Furniss commenced a work which has been wonderfully blessed of God. There are now

seven assemblies with a total membership of approximately 1,200. Along with Mr Graham he gave help in the coach work, and in conducting tent meetings. He was used of God to interest Mr and Mrs A. Clarke in the work in that needy land; they too have been blessed and made a blessing. Mr Graham wrote of his appreciation of Mr Castles, how he cared for him when he first arrived in Uruguay, taking him into his home and then engaging him in tract distribution, etc.; he added, "He was a real plodder".

Mrs Castles did not enjoy good health as her nervous system was upset from time to time. At times Mr and Mrs Graham had her in their home so as to give Mr Castles some opportunity to relax and rest. It was when they were home on furlough, she went to be with the Lord. He then returned alone and lived in the rooms at the Gospel hall, which had earlier been a disused school. After some time he returned to Belfast and resided in Agincourt Avenue. He quietly moved amongst the saints, manifesting a Christ-like spirit, encouraging them in the work of the gospel, and seeking to strengthen assembly testimony. In the spring of 1943, he suffered a stroke and went home to be "with Christ". He was buried in Belfast, leaving behind a fragrant testimony to the grace and keeping power of God.

MR ALEXANDER CLARKE
1912-1985

Mr Clarke was born in Belfast on November 1st, 1912, but when he was only a few months old his family went to live in Dublin, where he was brought up. When he was eighteen years old he was saved, and after baptism was received into the fellowship of Merrion Hall assembly, which was then a large assembly and a great light amidst the darkness of that lovely city. He became involved in the open-air work in the centre of the city, which was faithfully carried on despite opposition from quite a number of parties. Mr Clarke also associated with the 'Gospel Coach' work, when each Saturday, towns and villages were visited and the gospel made known. Each Lord's Day he visited the 'Union' where there were many aged and ailing people and there, again preached Christ.

In 1939 he was married in Merrion Hall, to Miss Sheila Paul and in 1946 they were commended by the Merrion Hall assembly to the work in Uruguay. The early years were spent in learning the language and endeavouring to adapt to a different culture. He was linked with Mr Mills from New Zealand, working on the Bible Coach and often staying away from home for many months, distributing literature and preaching in the open-air—often in places where the gospel had never been preached. God blessed these efforts and souls were won for Christ. Later he worked with two business men who gave much time to the gospel—Mr Conaty and Mr Boyd; also with Mr Goodson, another New Zealand worker, as well as at times being with Mr D. Thompson, a fellow Irishman. He encouraged

local brethren to engage in the gospel and often enjoyed sharing meetings with them.

In later years he paid visits to the Argentine giving help in many of the assemblies. The need of small assemblies in Uruguay weighed heavily with him and much time was spent teaching and shepherding the saints in isolated places. At other times he went to Paraguay and gave appreciated help in the work of the 'Launch'—reaching many by means of the waterways.

On the 29th August, 1985, after 39 years of diligent and fruitful labour, God called His servant home. Many believers from different assemblies came to the hall where his body lay, and some stayed all night to be of comfort and help to his widow. The funeral was to the British Cemetery; Mr Vallejo and Mr Sora spoke in the hall and Mr Barris gave a message at the graveside. Mrs Clarke continues to stay in Uruguay.

MR JOHN CRAIG
1890-1976

Mr Craig was born in Cloghogue, County Antrim, in December, 1890. When he was very young his family moved to Belfast and in that city he was brought up. His family attended a Presbyterian Church, where he first learned the Scriptures and was taught to reverence God. He was invited to hear Mr Tom Rea, a well-known Irish Evangelist, who was having meetings in a large tent in the city. At these meetings his brother got saved and John was awakened to see he needed salvation. He carefully read the Bible and became very conscious of God's holiness and his own unworthy condition, and longed to be right with God. His brother was able to explain God's ways to him and from John 3:16 he had the light and assurance of salvation.

In a few weeks he was baptised and received into the assembly then meeting in Comber Place, and, later called Ebenezer, Oldpark Road, Belfast. He became involved in children's work and open-air witness, and engaged with 'the village workers' in carrying the gospel to the villages and small towns convenient to Belfast. The young men of that group were all gospel-minded and keen students, and John, like them, really loved his Bible. In early christian life Romans 12:1-2, by the Spirit's power, reached his heart and as long as life lasted controlled his conduct.

Hearing Mr G.M.J. Lear speak about the need of South America, he felt this was where God would have him to be. During the 1914-1918 war, it was not possible for him to get a passport to Argentina, so he usefully occupied the time of waiting in Bible study, as well as learning Spanish

26

and other matters that became very useful when he arrived in South America. When he told his boss at the factory, he was at once offered promotion, a house to live in and excellent prospects for the future. His employer could not understand a young man leaving everything in Ireland to go to a foreign land, and without a salary.

In 1919 he worked for the last day in secular employment and, giving his mother his last salary, stepped out in faith to serve the Lord. His brethren heartily gave him a letter of commendation, which he honoured and carefully kept all his life. Spending a short time in England, he sought the company and counsel of well-known brethren who helped and encouraged him. He arrived in Buenos Aires early in 1919, met by Mr Jenkins, who took him that evening to distribute tracts and invite people to tent meetings. From that evening until his home-call in 1976 he was a consistent labourer; like another great servant: "publickly, and from house to house".

For about 9 years he worked with Mr Drake with a printing press at Quilmes, going to preach at night in Bernae, Wilde, Berazategui and Laplata. His first wife was an Argentinian girl, who was a member of the assembly at Quilmes. They had three children, but when these were very young their mother died. After a few years he remarried; this time a lady who was a missionary in Argentina became his wife and together they served in Buenos Aires. During 1946 he came to Ireland on his second furlough. For health reasons his wife remained in Argentina and while in Ireland he had the sad news that she had been taken to be with the Lord.

In 1949 Mr Morris invited him to the work in the province of Chubut at Trevelin, while the Morris family went to Wales on furlough. He agreed to go but, when the day came for him to undertake the three-day train journey, he had no money for his fare. Still he felt he should go, and taking his luggage with him, en route to the station, he called at the post office. There awaiting him was a letter with enough money for his ticket. A remarkable thing about it was that never before or since had he any fellowship from that brother.

In 1950 he married Miss Nest Evans, whose parents were Welsh. In 1947 she had been commended to gospel work amongst women and children, and together they had twenty-six happy years in the gospel. A number of years were spent in Chubut building up a work commenced by a native worker. As John was getting on in years, he felt the burden and earnestly prayed for fellow workers. God answered his prayer, and in 1966 a young couple from Buenos Aires joined him and together they saw spiritual prosperity and blessing. John was an acceptable gospel preacher, who could also minister to the saints. He was a humble man who was often seen painting the hall, washing the floor and making tea at meetings; no job was too menial for him. He had a wise head and a shepherd's heart.

His closing years were spent in Trelew. Early in 1974 he had a stroke and although in a little while he recovered somewhat and commenced a Bible Reading in his home, it was evident 'his natural strength was abated'. He went to be "with Christ" on 25th September, 1976. A native evangelist looking at his still form said, "Good and faithful servant". Fifty-seven years were completed for God and His work. He was buried in Trelew.

MR SAMUEL W. CURRAN
1921-1987

Mr Curran was born in Banbridge on 9th December, 1921, the eldest of a family of four boys. His father, Mr Robert Curran, was an evangelist who laboured in the North of Ireland. Sam was saved in 1938 at meetings conducted in Banbridge by Messrs Stewart and Bingham. He was baptised and received into the local assembly. From early christian life he interested himself in the study of the Scriptures and helping where he could in children's meetings, open-air preaching and tract distribution. The compiler has happy memories of early youth, when Sam and he cycled together to speak at Sunday evening meetings.

He was interested in wood-work and spent some time in joinery work as well as two years in antique furniture work. This training was valuable to him in Brazil where he made seats, platforms and helped to build gospel halls. He was married in 1944 to Miss Eleanor M. Alexander, who was in fellowship in the Newcastle assembly.

In 1958 he with his wife and family sailed for Brazil; quite a large step at his age. He was heartily commended by the assemblies at Ahorey, Newcastle and Banbridge. They spent the first 1½ years in Porto Alegre, using Mr John McCann's home—he was on furlough at that time. He attended classes for language study and quickly got a good grasp of Portuguese. He became proficient in the language and with ease and profit could preach and teach.

In 1960 he moved to Osorio and made his home there, until he was taken to Heaven in 1987. God blessed his

earnest labours and souls were saved and God's people led in "paths of righteousness". The assembly at Capivari, which currently has about forty in fellowship, was formed as the result of his work. He laboured harmoniously with his fellow missionaries, Messrs McCann, Wilson, Watterson, Wright, Matthews and Glenn, as well as having happy and fruitful times with native workers, Jose Mattos, Senhor Alegio and others. On 24th July, 1987 a tape recording of his mother's funeral reached him; she had died six weeks earlier. Listening to it he said, "That was very well done, I liked that"; later in that day he left for the last gospel meeting of a series of seven weeks. His message was based on some of the "trumpets" of Scripture, with special emphasis on 1 Corinthians 15:52. At that series of meetings he gave out almost every night, the same hymn— one verse roughly translated would be:

Oh that I might see Jesus my Saviour
There in that beautiful city of which He is the light;
There with His redeemed participate in that glory
Love Him, adore Him and never sin again.

Arriving home after that meeting and discussing recent happenings, particularly the sudden death of Mr W. Glenn, he said, "There is a nice new cemetery outside of town, that would certainly do for me". That night he didn't sleep much as a severe pain in his back troubled him. In the morning he arranged to have some medical attention and before leaving typed a letter to Mr G. Buchanan, who was preparing to leave Ireland and serve the Lord in Brazil. Brother Buchanan had said something in a letter to him about the big and costly step it was. Sam in his reply said, "Yes, we know from experience it is, but then there was nothing too costly for the Son of God, in order to have the like of us with Him for ever".

While speaking at the service before Mr Glenn's body left Brazil, he quoted and read Isaiah 54:10, both in Portuguese and English, no doubt with a view to helping and comforting Mrs Glenn; "For the mountains shall depart, and the hills be removed; but my kindness shall not depart from thee, neither shall the covenant of my peace be removed, saith the Lord that hath mercy on thee". When in a few days he suddenly passed away, the words were a blessing to his wife and family.

His life was not without its sorrows. He experienced great sadness when he lost two grown-up sons inside ten months, one in a car accident, the other through illness. Friends could see this left lasting marks upon him, but he bravely carried on with his work. He was a wise, balanced man, with convictions which were strong concerning assembly matters and God's work, but he could also see others who were sincere and while he may not have agreed with them, he manifested a spirit of grace and helpfulness. His ministry was conducive to harmony and unity. His appearance would have made folk think he was austere and severe, but, behind that solemn countenance, he had a strong sense of humour. In Brazil and when in Ireland on furlough, the saints rejoiced to see him rise at a conference; they would get something worthwhile, in a way they could readily understand.

The believers in Brazil and Ireland were shocked and deeply saddened at the death of such a useful missionary and a brother beloved. His wishes were carried out, and he was buried in Osorio, with Messrs Matthews, Watterson and Orr sharing in the services.

DR P.K. DIXON
1898-1955

Dr Dixon was born in September 1898; he was saved in early life and in fellowship in Merrion Hall, Dublin. Finishing his medical studies, he laid aside earthly prospects and decided to serve the Lord in Africa. In 1926 he married Miss O.P. Archer, a member of a well-known, highly-respected Dublin family; she was also in fellowship in Merrion Hall. In 1926 they were both commended by the Merrion assembly to the work of the Lord in the Congo. He obtained permission from the Belgian government to practise medicine there, and, while this occupied much of the time, his great desire was to use it as a means of getting the gospel to the people.

For a short time he resided in Bunkeya, later deciding to go to Chibambo at Kasenga on the Luapula river. In this area he served for thirty years, taking only four brief periods of leave outside Central Africa during that time, and on each occasion he gave his leisure to further medical study. In 1934, he became an F.R.C.S. (Ireland). Realising the immense suffering caused by eye diseases in the tropics, he devoted himself specially to this branch of medicine. His published researches, especially in the field of trachoma, led to his recognition as an outstanding authority in ophthalmology. His work was recognised by the Belgian government, when he was decorated by the King of the Belgians.

In 1927 his wife 'fell asleep', having been ill for some time. About the same period he was mauled by a lion while in camp and sustained severe injuries, the effects of which

34

he was to endure for the remainder of his life. At that time he returned to the UK for treatment, after which he went to India to gain experience of eye diseases before returning to the Congo in 1929, where he married Miss I.H. Russell, a nurse who was then working in that area. At Chibambo, there had been a small dispensary (9 feet by 12 feet); medical cases received their medicine at the window, private cases were attended to inside and ordinary ulcer patients sat on a log in the open. A very much larger building was erected, with operating theatre, laboratory and rooms for 'in patients'. Contrasting the conditions, Dr Dixon said, "When one has had to stop and cover the wound with one's hands because of an approaching dust storm, or endure a continuous spray of 'flit' because of flies, one appreciates the vast improvement". He thanked the Lord who had provided all this, through His people. Many patients testified to hearing the gospel and getting to know the Saviour while there.

Constant ill health eventually forced him to leave the Luapula Valley. He spent a year as a medical officer at Nkana mine, going in 1953 to the Government African Hospital in Lusaka. Whilst doing the duties of surgical specialist, he continued to make known the gospel. It was in this hospital he passed to be with the Lord on April 21st, 1955, and was buried in Lusaka.

MR HERBERT DOUGLAS
1896-1935

In the years following the first world war, missionary interest was keen in the Lurgan district, in some measure due to the exercise of the esteemed Dr. Darling.

One of the young men who came under the doctor's influence was Bertie Douglas. He was the youngest of a family whose parents were God-fearing and spiritual. In 1916, he left home to join the British army. When leaving Guildford, about to entrain with hundreds of others, a young lady offered him a copy of John's gospel. He put it in his tunic pocket, later to read it and be saved. Possibly that young lady never heard of his conversion, but her good work was blessed and she will be rewarded, "God is not unrighteous to forget", Heb. 6:10.

While travelling in the train, he read the Scriptures and wrote later to his mother to tell her he had accepted Christ and was saved. He said, "John 5:24 made me think deeply; reading on I came to chapter 7, verses 33-34; so deep was my concern I felt it was now or never. Pray for me that I may have strength to continue".

When the war ended and he had returned to civilian life, he became identified with the Lurgan assembly as well as sharing in the gospel activities of the Bleary and Kilmore assemblies. Early in life he was seen to have a shepherd's heart and showed a special care for young men. When he went abroad to serve the Lord, one of them said, "We felt like orphans". Our brother Mr J.E. Fairfield tells of his first visit to Lurgan Gospel Hall; noting he was a stranger Bertie approached him and asked for his name, then said, "I'm

Bertie Douglas, let us walk home together". Mr Fairfield adds, "That friendship continued as long as Bertie lived and was as warm as it was true".

In 1923 the Lurgan assembly, joined by the surrounding assemblies, heartily commended him to the Lord's work in Venezuela. He quickly adapted himself to the new surroundings and learned the language. He became useful in the gospel and later in ministering the Word amongst the assemblies. He was married in Venezuela to Miss A. McMeekin of Ahoghill, County Antrim, who was a true helpmeet and was loyally by his side until God called him home. God blessed them with two children.

After his marriage he settled in San Felipe and saw a good work that was solid and stood the test of years. He shared in gospel work with Mr Saword, Mr Williams, Mr Fletcher and others. In 1929 when Mr J. Wells went out, he made his home with Bertie and his wife, as did Mr Fairfield when he went out in 1933.

He had a cheery disposition, and his bright smiling countenance with a sociable manner fitted him to gain favour with the people. This, with a real sense of God's presence, made him one who was signally blessed to many.

He suffered a great deal from successive attacks of malaria and on account of indifferent health returned to Northern Ireland on furlough in 1935. Instead of resting, as many felt he should, he engaged in gospel work, as well as giving reports of the work in Venezuela. Despite being unwell, he left his bed to keep an appointment in Ballyclare, which proved to be his last meeting. He contracted pleurisy, from which double pneumonia developed and on 31st October, 1935 he went home to glory, from the house of his father-in-law Mr Robert McMeekin.

The funeral was from Ahoghill to Shankill Cemetery, Lurgan. Amidst manifestations of sorrow, believers from all over the province attended, and places of business closed as the funeral procession passed through Lurgan town.

Mr J. Stewart and Mr W. McCracken conducted the service in Ahoghill. Mr J. Diack spoke at the graveside service, basing his message on Acts 11:24. After Mr H. Baillie prayed, the large company sang the hymn:

"For ever with the Lord!"
Amen, so let it be;
Life from the dead is in that word,
'Tis immortality.

MR FRED ENGLISH
1908-1976

Mr English was born at Ballynabraggett, County Down on 17th July, 1908, the eldest of a family of three, whose parents were both christians. When Fred was fifteen his father died and, about that time, he was saved at meetings held by Mr R. Curran. From the very beginning of his christian experience he took a keen interest in spiritual things. He would rise very early in the morning to spend time with God and his Bible, then help his mother around the little farm, before going off to work in the linen factory at Donacloney.

It was quite a usual thing for him to get home after 6 p.m., have a meal and then cycle many miles to preach the gospel. Despite weather conditions he would do this for six or seven weeks, a feature of gospel work in Ireland! In these efforts souls were saved and it became increasingly evident that God was using him and training him for future service.

Toward the close of World War II, he went to work in Belfast as a bread server, lodging with a christian couple who were in fellowship in Apsley Street Assembly. The lady of the house later speaking about Fred said, "He was so good, he was transparent"; this was so true, "an Israelite indeed, in whom was no guile". At that time he associated with Apsley Street Assembly, and, as was the bent of his life, he put his all into the things of God. He was a man of prayer and at any time when free from daily toil would be found alone upon his knees with an open Bible.

God was guiding him and making it clear that he should

devote his life to the work of the gospel. For a short time he considered Japan, but that door closed and he became convinced he should go to South Africa. When he approached his home assembly at Waringstown, they were not at all surprised and, with neighbouring assemblies, they heartily commended him to the grace of God.

While awaiting a ship for South Africa, he joined Mr S.W. Lewis, a pioneer in border areas of the Irish Republic and gave valuable help, with God's blessing. Upon arriving in Cape Town in June 1946, he was met and welcomed by Mr S.H. Moore, whose company he had for only one week as Mr Moore was returning to Ireland on furlough. He rented a room and took up studies in the Afrikaans language, at the same time engaging in nightly gospel meetings in English-speaking areas.

In 1947, Miss Doreen Wylie, to whom Fred was engaged before leaving for Africa, commended by the Ebenezer Assembly, Belfast, went out to join him. They were married a week after she arrived in the Cape.

Fred said he had no desire to remain where assemblies and workers were, "not to build upon another man's foundation", but to reach out to "the regions beyond"; a laudable desire. So in 1949, he and his wife left Cape Town and went into the country to Worcester where assembly activities were unknown. For quite a while they found it very difficult, as there was much religious opposition. So hard was the going, that at one point Fred was heard to say, "Let us go home and cry defeat". But just then God came in—one Saturday evening after preaching in a village, a man followed him and asked if he would come back and preach again.

In this village God worked and an assembly was formed. Their first breaking of bread was in primitive conditions, with chickens, etc., running amongst their feet as they remembered the Lord. The people were very poor, and only one woman could read, but God's presence was real and sweet. Some of the believers experienced bitter opposition, being forced from their homes and places of employment, but God honoured them and undertook for them. They were able to get work and houses in nearby

Worcester, where they formed the nucleus of the assembly. They hired a hall and, although opposition continued, the work grew and others were saved and added to the testimony. Apart from the Lord's Day meetings, for some years the assembly gatherings were in the homes of the christians. In these areas and in the mountain villages Fred travelled and carried the gospel, his pioneer spirit taking him to where the gospel had never been preached. A work was commenced in Robertson and an assembly formed.

In 1961, Fred's health was not very good and his doctor advised him to have a visit home to Ireland. He was only ten days at home when he collapsed and was unable to be out at meetings for eight months. After eighteen months, when he had recovered from the effects of the stroke, he felt he would like to return to his field of labour. Though a sick and weak man he put his remaining strength into gospel work. He could be seen night after night with his tilley lamp going up into the mountains to hold a meeting. Many more were saved, other assemblies formed, two halls were built and several outposts started. From one of these assemblies, a couple have been commended to the work of the Lord.

On the 9th February, 1976, Fred and his wife had just left their daughter at Stellenbosch for her first term at the university, when, within half an hour he suffered a massive heart attack and was with the Lord he loved and served so faithfully. His funeral was from Parown Gospel Hall, and was very large, folks attending from as far away as Durban and Johannesburg. His missionary brethren S. Moore, G. Anderson, and K. Elliott, assisted by local brethren shared in the funeral services. A coach load of coloured saints from Worcester and Robertson sang at the graveside the hymn, "It is only till He come" in the Afrikaans language. Thus was laid to rest a devoted, honourable self-effacing man. His widow remained in South Africa, his children and their partners are both in assembly fellowship.

MR JAMES GEDDIS

1892-1956

Mr Geddis was born in Lurgan on 8th July, 1892. Under the preaching of Mr John Moneypenny he and his mother were saved on 8th January, 1905 and after baptism they were received into the Lurgan assembly. The saints there took an interest in James and with their help and encouragement he developed spiritually. He was given a class in the Sunday school and later had the joy of seeing them all saved. He was actively engaged in gospel preaching around much of the Lurgan district.

He was married in 1919 to Miss Edith McNeill, who was in the Bleary assembly, and God blessed the union with four children. Soon after their first child was born they were commended to the Lord's work in Africa and sailed in complete dependence upon God, who faithfully cared for them as long as life lasted. The ship docked at Cape Town and from there they had a long train journey of five days and nights until they reached Kamboue in the Belgian Congo, now Zaire. There was a party of seven met by Mr Gavin Mowat, who assisted them to their respective spheres of labour.

Mr Geddis settled in Kalunda, building a mud brick house and making furniture as well as learning the Lunda language, in which he became fluent and could preach and teach with acceptance and blessing. His labours were fruitful and many were saved, some being added to the assembly at Kalunda, and in new districts assemblies were formed. There was a good deal of opposition and, in some cases, severe persecution. It became so bad that in 1937, he

45

decided to move across the border into Northern Rhodesia, now Zambia. He built a house at Dipalata and commenced a work there, where he was warmly welcomed by Chief Ishinde and his people. Chief Ishinde's son is a saved man and in assembly fellowship. Quite a number of the believers from Kalunda followed him into Rhodesia and were of help in this new work. In 1939, the assembly was formed and a good hall erected, soon after which, they left for a furlough in Northern Ireland. Twenty-four days was the time it took them to get to Livingstone to board a train for Cape Town. There Mr Geddis took ill and it was several weeks before they could sail for the UK. During the voyage, war broke out and it was with a real sense of thanksgiving they safely docked in England. They could not return to Africa during the war, and in those years he lived in Bangor and was fully engaged in gospel preaching and ministry of the Word. Souls were saved and saints were helped. It was during that period the compiler of this book, heard him give an address on Deuteronomy 33:16— "The good will of Him that dwelt in the bush", which made profitable and permanent impressions.

He was a man of sincere and strong convictions, who was prepared to do what he believed to be God's will, irrespective of the favour or frown of others. During the time he lived in Bangor and was speaking of the great need in Africa, a number of others became exercised about it and were commended by their assemblies to help in the work. In 1946, he and his family, with a number of others, left the UK for Dipalata. The native believers with many local folk met them and rejoiced for their presence with them again. Soon he was back "into harness" and busy in the gospel, seeing others saved and further assemblies formed. In 1987 a jubilee conference was held at which two thousand were present, to thank God for His goodness and to listen to the ministry of the Word.

In 1950, due to illness, Mrs Geddis was advised by the doctor to return to Ireland for medical attention. In 1951 they returned to Dipalata, where it was noticed that Mr Geddis was not so strong and was slowing up quite a bit. However, he had an exercise to build a new hall as the old one was ravaged by termites, and, during this work, he suffered a slight heart attack. In 1956 he developed a terminal illness, and soon he became aware that the end was near. He was bright and happy and repeatedly said, "They talk about the terrors of death, I know nothing about that, it is home sweet home". He asked that Revelation 5 be read at his funeral and that the people be told of the blood of Christ. He also requested that those he laboured with would be responsible for his funeral services. Messrs Logan, Halliday, Arnot and McQuillan, as well as two African elders took part at the very large funeral, some having travelled long distances to pay tribute to a beloved brother in Christ. His widow continued in Dipalata until her homecall in November, 1964. They are buried side by side in the forest, a little way out from Dipalata.

MR W. GIBSON
1894-1978

Mr Gibson was born in Lanaglug, Coagh, County Tyrone, on the 23rd September, 1894. His father engaged in some farming as well as some house building work. He was saved in 1913, when Mr J.T. Dickson and Mr J. Stewart had Gospel Meetings in his district, and soon afterwards he was received into the assembly at Aughavey. While still quite young, he emigrated to Canada and found employment in Eaton's large stores. He was active and helpful in the assembly at Hamilton, Ontario, and this assembly commended him to the work of the Lord in Guyana in 1919. Six months later he was married to Miss Grace Lawson, who was in fellowship in the Hamilton assembly. After a term of service there, they went on furlough to Canada, where they met Mr Charles Leonard who encouraged them to visit the West Indies, which they did. In 1926 he commenced tent meetings and saw great blessing in large meetings and many being saved. William's practice was to teach the converts, form an assembly and then reach out to other districts; very much in keeping with apostolic ways of working.

In 1929 he saw the Maranatha assembly formed. It has grown to be very large and at one time 700 were in fellowship. This has been a centre of much activity and from it missionaries, evangelists, and teachers have gone forth to be of blessing in other spheres. Mr Gibson laboured with quite a number of others who have each been blessed of God—Mr and Mrs Hatley, Mr and Mrs F. Fenton, Mr and Mrs S. Calcraft, Mr and Mrs G. Hale, Mr

and Mrs H. Wildish, Mr E. Willie, and others 'whose names are in the book of life'. These dear brethren saw God at work in a remarkable way, in souls being saved, lives transformed and assemblies planted. In the years between 1850 and 1860, J.N. Darby and G.V. Wigram visited the islands and saw assemblies formed. Alexander Marshall and quite a number of earnest preachers and business men contributed to the development and growth of assembly work. It is estimated that there are around 70 assemblies in Jamaica with around 5,000 believers in fellowship, 200 Sunday schools reaching thousands of children each week, and 60 or more Jamaican brethren in full-time service locally, while others have gone further afield.

In 1963 his wife Grace, a true helpmeet, died, and in 1964 he married Amy Karram, who faithfully cared for him while his life lasted. In 1974 he was ill and his mental faculties were weakening. His wife required surgery, and so they returned to Canada. William was admitted to hospital, where he spent four years, having suffered two strokes. In July 1978 he was called to be with the Lord, after 55 years of dedicated and fruitful service. At the large funeral, Mr B. Black, a convert of Mr Gibson's in earlier years, paid a fitting tribute. Mr A. Henrignes from Olivet Gospel Hall in Jamaica gave the address and the company joined in singing, "Face to face shall I behold Him". His sons also shared in the services in the funeral parlour and at the graveside.

His father in the faith, Mr J. Stewart, said, "I may not have had many spiritual children from the meetings in 1913, but I have had many spiritual grandchildren and most of them coloured!"

MR WILFRED GLENN
1938-1987

Mr Glenn was born in Leverogue in 1938, the fifth of a family of nine; his parents were farmers and in fellowship in the assembly at Ballymagarrick. Wilfred was saved when twelve years of age, at the close of a Lord's Day evening meeting, at which Mr A. Caulfield had spoken. Soon he was baptised and received into the assembly. Early in christian life he manifested real interest in Divine matters, helping in children's work and anxious to further the spread of the gospel.

He helped local brethren in Lord's Day evening meetings and shared with Mr F. Knox and others in special series of meetings. After his marriage in 1967 to Miss Kathleen Crawford, he made his home at Glengormley. In the assembly there he heartily engaged in all the activities and was really useful and highly esteemed. When he made known his exercise regarding Brazil, the saints were very happy and, while sorry to lose his help, they heartily commended him to the work of the Lord.

In 1970 he left for Brazil, having had the right hand of fellowship extended to him from the Glengormley assembly. In Brazil he made his first home in Candelaria. After learning the language, he joined first of all with Mr John McCann, who had been in the country from 1948. After two years he moved to live in Sao Gabriel, remaining there until the Lord took him home.

He was a diligent worker and laboured with Messrs H. Wilson, S. Curran, T. Matthews, T. Wright and T. Meekin; all of these were his fellow country-men. He also worked

with at least two Brazilian evangelists, Jose Cipriano and Jose Mattos. His pleasant manner gave him favour with the people and he was successful in getting many to hear the gospel. He had the joy of seeing the assembly formed at Sao Gabriel, as well as seeing souls saved in quite a number of other places.

While he had several severe illnesses and operations, he was strong-minded and had a large measure of 'stickability'. When home on his last furlough, instead of taking some rest, he gave missionary reports in Ireland and Scotland. He also engaged in several series of gospel meetings, joining with Mr S. McBride and Mr W. Bingham, God giving blessing in salvation. He was in the midst of a series of meetings with Mr T. Wright, when he took seriously ill and, despite careful medical attention, he suddenly passed away on 17th July, 1987.

His family arranged for his body to be brought to Ireland for burial. When the Brazilian brethren were asked regarding this, they replied saying, "His family gave him to us to preach the gospel, it is only reasonable we should give him back to them". A short service was conducted in Brazil, at which Mr S. Curran, Mr T. Wright, and Mr T. Matthews took part. Mr Wright accompanied the widow and two small children on the journey home. The funeral took place from Glengormley Gospel Hall, which was filled to overflowing. Messrs J. Moore, H. Wilson, E. Fairfield, and J.G. Hutchinson shared in the service. The body was interred at Ballycairn, beside his parents, Messrs A. McShane, A. Caulfield and T. Wright taking part in the service.

His life was short—only forty-nine years, yet it was felt he had put much into it for God. His widow has decided to remain in Brazil and do what she can for God.

MR H. WINFIELD GRAHAM
1905-1986

Mr Graham was born in the city of Londonderry on the 9th April, 1905. His father was in the insurance business, and, when Winfield was 2 years old, the family moved into Muff, County Donegal. Upon leaving school he got a situation in the Belfast Banking Company and went to work in Belfast. He was invited to a gospel meeting in the city, conducted by the well-known evangelist, Mr W.P. Nicholson; that night in 1922, he got saved. For four years he carefully studied the Scriptures to discover God's path for him. Learning the truths of baptism, breaking of bread, and assembly fellowship, he was received into Adam Street assembly, Belfast. As long as life lasted these truths and this pathway were dear to him and to them he adhered steadfastly. Early in life he manifested the zeal and fervour of an Evangelist, and it was no surprise to his brethren when he made known his desire to serve the Lord abroad. In 1929 he gave up a promising career in the banking world, and, taking a job with a railway company, he was granted permission to live in Uruguay.

Soon after settling in the country, he left his employment in the railway and until 1986 was a faithful servant of God. In 1930 he was married to Miss M.J. Thompson from Kilmore, County Tyrone, and together they lived in Las Piedras. She had been nursing in Londonderry and was commended by that assembly. From the time he stepped out to serve the Lord in a full-time way, he never had a home in Uruguay. He got a canvas tent sent out from Ireland and in this he and his wife lived for many years in

the interior of the country. At that time it was not difficult to get a site for the tent and often a vacant home nearby. They carried with them a simple outfit of camp beds, folding chairs, a small cooker heated by a primus stove, and other utensils.

When they pitched their tent in Rocha and commenced meetings, they found a number waiting for the gospel; some were soon saved and an assembly formed. In another small town, Blas Bon1río, meetings were held and another assembly was commenced.

This was the pattern and result of the work over the years. A brother from Argentina (an Italian by birth) joined them; later a young Uruguayan couple, C. Rojas and his wife Carmen, were their helpers for some years.

In 1952 he returned to Ireland, having had only one furlough since going out. He settled in County Donegal, living in a caravan until 1972, when they were able to rent a house in Strabane, where they remained until his decease in 1986. In all their married life this was their first house; he had a truly pilgrim spirit. The years in Donegal and Strabane were spent in consistent gospel work in fairs, open-air meetings, and mostly in isolated places. He became a well-known figure, displaying gospel texts, giving away gospel literature, somtimes with the help of local believers, but often alone. He never sought prominence and was content to serve God, even in obscurity.

Between 1964 and 1971 he made four short visits to South America, giving ministry and encouragement as opportunity afforded. The Spanish-speaking christians remember with gratitude his excellent translation of the hymn, "Thou art the everlasting word".

During late 1985 and for the months of 1986 until his home-call, his health was not good and it was evident that his race was almost run. He was taken into Faith House, the assembly home for aged saints, and a week later, on 2nd October, 1986, suddenly passed away. Earlier he had made request regarding his funeral and this was carried out. He was buried from the Strabane Gospel Hall; the brethren from Londonderry assembly, Messrs Hanna, Hartley, Armstrong and McClean, taking the services. His widow is currently in a retirement home in Londonderry city.

MR F.W. HALLETT

1882-1947

Mr Fred. W. Hallett was born in Dublin on 30th June, 1882, and was commended by the assembly at Merrion Hall, Dublin, to the work in Angola, Africa, in September 1913. He accompanied Mr and Mrs Edward Sanders to Chilonda in Bié, where he spent six years among the Umbundu speaking people.

A number of the workers in Angola had been exercised about a thickly-populated area on the banks of the Lungwebungo river in the southern part of the country. It had been visited by Messrs F.T. Lane and Francis Figg from Bié and later by James MacPhie from Cazombo. The people were a mixture of Chokwes, Lovales and Luchazes. In 1918, Messrs William Maitland and Herbert Griffiths from Boma in Chokweland spent some weeks in the area. When Mr Hallett returned from his first furlough in 1922, hearing of the need, he went into the interior from Bié and settled at Luonze on the Lungwebungo river. Mr Maitland stayed with him for some time and together they started a new pioneer work. It was the most southerly of the assembly mission centres in Angola.

Miss Manders, also from Merrion Hall, Dublin, spent some years at Luonze and later went to Bulawayo in Rhodesia where she did a valuable work. Miss Edith Howell, who had been commended from U.S.A., went to Luonze from Buila in Chokweland and after a short visit died there of blackwater fever. She was the first missionary to give her life for the Lord in that area.

Mr Albert Horton and his wife Petronella commended

from Buffalo, New York, visited Luonze for a year to help out in the early days of the work. At that time Mr Hallett was alone, isolated by hundreds of miles from the nearest civilisation. Mr Horton gives a graphic account of conditions and their experiences in his book, *Africa, Oh Africa.*

Mr Hallett was married on July 12th, 1927 at Chavuma, Northern Rhodesia (now Zambia). His wife, Winnifred Gertrude Anderson, was a school teacher, who had come to Africa to teach the children of missionaries. Together they settled into the work at Luonze and for many years did a faithful service for the Lord. The record is on high. Their only son Arthur who was born in 1935, and his wife Christine are commended missionaries, resident in Harare, the capital of Zimbabwe. For years Arthur laboured in Moçambique, now called Maputo, and still pays extended visits to that country.

Mr Hallett died in October 1947 as the result of an accident and is buried at Luonze. The assembly there, as well as all the mission centres in Angola, have suffered severely in recent years owing to the civil war, but the work goes on. Thousands of the African believers have had to flee into neighbouring Zambia, but carry on a vibrant testimony there in the refugee camps. Mrs Hallett is now in the Green Pastures Retirement Home in Fishhoek, South Africa.

MR JOHN A. HEWITT

1907-1942

Mr Hewitt was born in 1907, the fourth member of a family of seven. His father was a farmer, as was John when he left school. He was saved in his early teenage years. Mr John Moneypenny had laboured much in the gospel in the district and his weighty gospel messages made lasting impressions on many. Soon after one of his visits John was saved. He so witnessed to the boys at school that none of them would sit or company with him, save W. Johnston, who later became his lifelong friend and who helped him in many ways ere he went to Japan.

He was for some time in the Ahorey assembly and later in Clonroot, where he engaged in Sunday school teaching. Miss E. Rountree, who serves the Lord in Africa, was one of his pupils. He was often found in the evening preaching to groups of the neighbours wherever he could get an audience. When he decided to go to Japan with the gospel, having been influenced by Mr R.J. Wright, his father was not happy and tried to discourage him by pointing out that there was property which would be his, if he remained at home, but, if he went away, it would go to others.

His brethren in Ahorey and Clonroot joined in his commendation and had a farewell meeting for him at which Mr E. Allen gave ministry and they wished him God's richest blessing. As he was about to board ship, he turned to his friend W. Johnston and said, "If you want that old vehicle of mine on the quay side, you can have it. If you want to see me again, you will have to come to Japan or wait until you get to heaven; I'll not be back." His father, at this

point, had relented, but John said, "As for my father, he doesn't know what he is talking about; I will not be back." Matthew 19:29 seemed to be his attitude.

When he arrived in Japan, he joined Mr Wright and settled in to study the language. At that time he wrote home saying, "How I long to be able to speak of Him— millions who have never heard of a Saviour's love." When able to use the language, he engaged in tract distribution, open-air preaching, and started a Sunday school in his own house. Shortly before the Japanese attack on Pearl Harbour, which brought America into the war, he was arrested and put in prison, after days of gruelling questions with relays of examiners. Many of the questions related to Emperor worship. John stedfastly refused to acknowledge 'the deity' of any human being, remaining loyal to Christ, his Lord and Master.

When arrested he was in excellent health and had money for his passage to Ireland, if needed. No account of this was ever given by the authorities. In a few weeks, according to police records, he was very ill and irrational. He was sent to Matsuzawa Byoin, Tokyo's insane asylum. But when the christians enquired about him, they could not find him. When, after the war, Mr Wright saw the medical report on him, it said, "He was not dangerous, simply singing hymns under his blanket." Mr Wright was strongly suspicious that certain experimental drugs had been tested on him and these caused the sudden deterioration of his health.

When some faithful christian ladies visited him, they were admitted to see him by an orderly, who against orders, received them. He was found lying on the floor chained. When he passed away the authorities would have arranged a Buddhist funeral, but God over-ruled and he had a christian funeral. Mr Wright, when repatriated, brought home his ashes and they were interred in Kilmore graveyard, where a large tombstone has the inscription:

John Alexander Hewitt
Missionary, who died in Japan 7th April, 1942,
And his ashes are interred here.
"Faithful unto death"

With a few Japanese saints and Mr Wright, John refused to join with the Japanese christian church under a government Minister of Religion, and steadfastly refused to worship any other than Christ. The cost was great, but the reward will be greater still, "A crown of life", Revelation 2:10.

MR JAMES E. JOHNSTON
1877-1950

Mr Johnston was born in Aghalee in 1877. When he was 20 years of age he was brought to know Christ as Saviour and gladly acknowledged Him as Lord. Those who knew him best testified to his increasing Christ-likeness as years passed. For some time he was in happy fellowship in the assembly at Adam Street, Belfast, from where he was commended to the work of the Lord in India in 1904.

When he arrived in India he joined with Mr W.N. Hearn, who had been there since 1888. They worked together at Karmatar, South Parganas and Bihar, engaging in village and camp work in the cool season. The assembly at Karmatar had about sixty in fellowship and here they would meet for the Lord's Day meetings. They had a number of preaching points where some of the believers lived and a great many in these parts heard the gospel and souls were saved.

Mr Johnston had a real love for the Indian people, and sought by life and lip to impress upon them the greatness of the love of God. They had many gods but knew nothing of a God of love, who had given His only Son to provide salvation for them. A younger missionary who accompanied him, wrote of how he was impressed with Mr Johnston's love for the local believers and how they reciprocated it. He was greatly respected as he would help them with their problems, and at times much patience and restraint were needed.

In 1911 he was married to Miss L.H. Watts at Banka, North India. She came from Hounslow, London, being

commended by a number of English assemblies. God blessed them with one daughter. Their home was in the same compound as that of Mr and Mrs Hearn, with whom they continued to labour. Mr Johnston devoted much time to working among Hindus, Mohammedans and some Aboriginal tribes, with a special interest in lepers.

Many believers were poor and needed assistance, which was given by Mr Johnston in a careful way, so that a feeling of too much dependence was not fostered. His tender care for many lepers was very marked as they came week by week. Medicine and rice were freely given as the gospel was preached. Many learned portions of scripture and he delighted in hearing them repeat the Scriptures. In his ministry Mr Johnston presented Christ and sought to have the attention of the hearers taken up with Him; his own Christ-likeness causing the ministry to have weight and effect. Fellow missionaries said, "His humility was genuine." Philippians 2:3 was so true of Him.

Due to famine conditions many children in the Rajputana states were left orphans. Mr H. Bird, with the help of others, brought many of these to mission stations in Bihar. Many got saved and Mr Johnston had the joy of teaching, guiding and encouraging these young people.

After forty-six years of devoted service, Mr Johnston returned to Ireland in 1950. Constant labour and care for others had taken their toll of his health, and after a short illness he died in the Royal Victoria Hospital on 25th May, 1950. He was buried from his nieces' home—his body was interred in Knockbreda Cemetery, the service being conducted by his life-long friends, Mr G. Watson and Mr D.L. Craig.

MR ALFRED LENNOX
1898-1981

Mr Lennox was born at Aughrim, County Londonderry in 1898, the youngest member of a farming family, whose parents were keen christians. In some respects, to the close of a long life, he retained the features of a 'son of the soil'. He attended the Rainey Endowed school in Magherafelt for the early part of his education, later going to Belfast, where he graduated as a pharmacist. It was during his time in Belfast, in 1916, that he got saved. He found employment in the south of Ireland, where he spent his spare time in making known the gospel in Counties Monaghan, Cavan and Longford. When on holiday, he rented an old school house near his home at Aughrim and in it conducted nightly gospel meetings.

In 1922 he emigrated to Canada making his home with an older brother in Toronto. Here he busied himself in gospel work, reaching out to areas around the city. Finding pharmacy unsatisfactory, he gave it up and went into the construction business in Timmons, North Ontario. Mr and Mrs Busby were living there and engaged in full-time gospel work. Throwing in his lot with this couple, Alfred was soon deeply involved in the assembly and much appreciated for his work amongst young and old.

In 1933, after much exercise, he decided to give up his lucrative business and, with the commendation of his brethren, go out into full-time service, in which he continued with consistency, consecration and courage, until the Lord took him home. For 12 years he pioneered in gold-mining towns and scattered farming communities, as

well as amongst lumber jacks and Indian settlements. It was difficult work and arduous because of the primitive conditions and extreme cold, but God blessed and souls were saved and assemblies formed. On one occasion, forty were baptised in a river, just before the severe winter set in. Another interesting happening was when a whole family of musicians got saved and with others broke bread for the first time in the dance hall they had formerly played in.

The severe weather and conditions affected his health and he was advised by his doctor to seek a warmer climate. In 1945 he arrived in the Windward Islands, where the missionary force had dwindled from more than a dozen, to two semi-retired widows and one sister who laboured in St Vincent. There were five assemblies there, with five in Grenada and three in Grenadines, all of which badly needed help. He was residing first of all in St George, Grenada, preaching the gospel, ministering to the saints and using his practical skill repairing Gospel halls.

In 1949 he returned to the UK on furlough and was invited to use the home of Mr and Mrs R. Scammell as a base whenever he was in the London area. Mr Scammell was a well-known evangelist. He made good use of the offer and eventually wooed and won Mr Scammell's daughter Ruth! They were married in 1950 and they went to the Windwards. God blessed the union with two daughters.

Until the girls were of school age, he resided in Grenada, frequently visiting the neighbouring islands. Then he moved to St Vincent where the education was not great due to the Roman Catholic influence. When it was time for higher education, Mrs Lennox brought the girls to England and made a home for them there; Mr Lennox continued alone. He was of a sturdy, independent nature and would let nothing hinder him in carrying out what he believed was the will of God.

He came to England for a short visit, hoping to return to his field of service, but God took him quite suddenly, thus bringing to a close a long and fruitful life. During a short stay in hospital in Ballymena a brother visiting him was exercised to give him a personal gift; his reaction was, "Brother, sincere thanks, but I don't really need it". Material things were by no means uppermost in his mind— "Godliness with contentment is great gain".

MR A. LOGAN
1908-1979

Mr Logan was born in Ballyclare, one of a family of five boys and two girls. He was saved when he was sixteen and received into the assembly at Ballyclare. He was engaged in the building trade, as a member of the family firm of W.M. Logan & Sons. From his youth he had a great interest in gospel work, and was known locally as 'the boy preacher', in company with others and particularly with Mr L. McIlwaine, who later went to Nova Scotia and did a good pioneer work. They had meetings in all kinds of places— tents, barns, hen houses, and open air; God giving them blessing, and thus encouraged they kept at it.

In 1931 he married Miss Margaret Hagan, a member of a family that had long and widespread association with assembly work in Ulster. They went to live in Carrickfergus, where he whole-heartedly put his best into the assembly, which was then small. Of recent years it has become a large assembly, meeting in a nice modern hall. As time went on he matured and became 'a pillar' in the assembly, at the same time continuing in gospel work. He was one of the few who were asked to preach the gospel in a service broadcast by the British Broadcasting Corporation, which he did with acceptance and blessing.

Upon taking early retirement from business, he felt constrained to devote the remainder of life to the work of the gospel. His wife had died earlier, leaving no family, so alone he set out for South Africa. He got a little apartment in Cape Town, and became actively engaged in preaching and teaching. While his brethren in Carrickfergus were

sorry to lose him, they heartily commended him and wished him God's blessing, which he experienced in a very real way.

For ten years he was busy amongst the people, particularly the coloured people, in whom he had a special interest. He gained their respect and love, and some even called their children after him. Souls were saved and the believers were edified and helped. He spoke of these years as being, "some of the happiest years of his life".

His death was sudden and unexpected as he appeared healthy and well, but God had seen his work was done. His family brought his body back to Ireland for burial. At the very large funeral in Carrickfergus, Mr T. Brown paid tribute on behalf of the Carrickfergus assembly. Mr J. Blair, and Mr T. Tughan gave appropriate messages and Mr R.J. Wright and Mr R. Wishart took part in prayer.

MR WILLIAM MAITLAND
1872-1960

William Maitland was born in County Antrim, Northern
Ireland on July 12th, 1872. In early life he emigrated to the
United States. We do not know the date or the
circumstances of his conversion, but he was in the
fellowship of the assemblies in Chicago and was commended
by them to missionary work in Central Africa in 1904. In
that year he accompanied Mr Arnot to Angola, along with
Mr Thomas Louttit, commended by the assembly in
Somerville, Mass, in Boston. After the usual difficulties of
transport from the West African coast into the interior,
they founded the work at Boma in Chokweland. Messrs
Maitland and Louttit were the first pioneer missionaries to
the Chokwe tribe. The Chokwes were a proud warlike
people who considered manual work to be beneath them. It
took years of patience and hard work to win their
confidence and learn their language, which at that time had
not been committed to writing. It was difficult to find
suitable food and in the early days Mr Maitland ate
something which was apparently poisoned. He hovered
between life and death for three weeks, and, although he
recovered, his digestion suffered from then until the end of
his life. After four years a few Chokwes professed
salvation, including a man called Sakachokwe, who later
became an outstanding leader and preacher among his own
people. War broke out between the Portuguese and the
Chokwe tribe in 1912. The Africans threatened to kill the
whites, including the missionaries, but they were defeated
and their morale broken. After this there was three years

of famine when many died of starvation, and the once proud Chokwes came to the missionaries begging for food. This was a turning point in the work. Over the years a number of honoured men and women came out from Britain, U.S.A., and Canada commended by the assemblies and these have spent their lives in dedicated and sacrificial service among the Chokwe people. As a result there has been an abundant harvest. To mention all the names and their labours would require a large volume.

In 1918, Mr Maitland and Mr Herbert Griffiths went to a well-populated area along the Lungwebungu river and preached the Gospel among Chokwe, Lovale and Luchaze people. Later Mr Fred. Hallett settled in the district at Luonze and Mr Maitland stayed with him for some time until the work was established. It was pioneering on virgin soil.

One of the most fruitful fields in Angola has been the diamond mine area at Dundo in the north-eastern part of the country. It is a completely indigenous work and no foreign missionary has ever received permission to live permanently in the area. In 1926 a number of African christians from Bié were sent there under forced labour contract regulations by the government. They took their Bibles and hymnbooks with them, but nothing was heard about them for several years. In 1931 Mr Maitland was in Saurimo where the Portuguese governor of the province was located. While at home on one of his furloughs, Mr Maitland had training in dentistry, and the governor, needing some dental work done, sent for him. He was so grateful to be relieved of his pain that he asked Maitland if he could do anything to express his gratitude. His only request was permission for him and his fellow missionaries to visit the christians in the diamond fields. This was granted with wonderful results. When the missionaries went in they found thousands of African believers who had been won for Christ and taught the Word by the original group of christians who had been sent there by force. That work continues until the present day. There are hundreds of assemblies, not only in the diamond fields at Dundo but in the surrounding tribal areas as well. It is a prime example of the work of the sovereign Spirit of God and the power of the Gospel.

Mr Maitland, broken in health, retired from the field in 1949. After a few years in the Western Assemblies Retirement Home in Claremont, California, where he was tenderly cared for, he entered into rest on 23rd October, 1960.

MR JAMES McCABE

1874-1957

Mr McCabe was born in Lower Darkley, Keady, County Armagh in April, 1874; his parents were farmers. He was saved in early life and associated with the assembly at Tullyglush, now known as Keady. Early in christian experience he took a keen interest in Divine matters, and dedicated himself to the Lord.

Like all his family, he was intelligent and possessed of an acute inquiring mind. He was an avid reader and acquired a wide knowledge of Holy Scripture, as well as a vast knowledge of things in general. While his village schooling did not extend to the classics, he taught himself a little Greek. In Bible readings and Ministry meetings he sought in a humble way to expound the Scriptures to the edification and profit of many. He led a very simple self-denying life; a relative who cared for him said, "He gave away almost all he received."

In 1896 he went to the Argentine where he joined Mr James Clifford and Mr and Mrs Langran at Tucuman. He also sought to help Mr and Mrs A. Jenkins and Miss Mohsler. In 1905 he went to Uruguay, making his home in Montevideo, where he laboured for two years. From 1907-1924 he was in Brazil, where he met and married Miss E.M. Harris, who was then teaching in Brazil. She was an English lady from Eltham, Kent. Little is recorded of these years of pioneer gospel work. Our brother was humble and self-effacing—when asked about Brazil, all he would say was, "I did a tiny little piece of work there." It is well 'the record is on high.' When he returned to the U.K. in 1925, he

79

lived in Bath and spent much time in village work, and from time to time visited his native Ulster. The closing years of his life were spent in Ulster, where he was much appreciated for his godly simplicity and the teaching of the Word.

When his health gave way, his daughter and her husband, Mr and Mrs Smith, who lived in the London area, cared for him with affection and tenderness until he was admitted to Lewisham General Hospital, where he passed away in October, 1957. He was buried in Hither Green Cemetery, London, Mr J.H. Large, former editor of Precious Seed magazine, conducting the funeral services.

When news of his death reached Belfast, a brother told a fellow-believer that Mr McCabe had gone to heaven; the other replied saying, "He hadn't far to go, he lived in close touch with it."

MR SAMUEL McCUNE

1886-1965

Mr McCune was born in Cardy, County Down. His parents were farmers and in fellowship in the Cardy assembly. The last time he preached the gospel was in Cardy Gospel Hall, and pointing to the back seat he said, "It was there in the Sunday school class I first heard the gospel."

He grew up in that district and although acquainted with the gospel did not get saved there. After his marriage to Miss Angus from Donaghadee, he went to live in Belfast where he built up a successful business in the construction industry. He was invited to gospel meetings in Bally-hackamore Gospel Hall, where Mr G. Wilson (later Dr. Wilson) was preaching. God was working and a number got saved, amongst them Mr and Mrs McCune. Soon afterwards they were received into the assembly, which was then a growing and happy company, and our brother felt very much at home and heartily engaged in its many activities.

Although he was happy in the assembly and successful in business, he felt God was calling him to devote his life to gospel work, which he did without a break until God called him home. The brethren in Ballyhackamore gladly agreed with his exercise and in 1925 'gave him the right hand of fellowship', commending him to the work of the Lord in the West Indies. Mr J. Turner spoke at his farewell meeting.

His early labours were in the Bahamas, then in Bermuda and Barbados, where God set the seal of His approval upon

his work in saving souls and forming assemblies. Often in later years our brother said, "The greatest joy of those years was to sit down with a little company to remember the Lord for the first time;" a happy experience he had on a number of occasions.

In the early 1930's, when many believers from what was then the British West Indies, went to work in the oil refineries of the Dutch islands, Aruba and Curacao, Mr McCune travelled with them to bring them together in assembly fellowship and to minister to their spiritual needs. After some years there, his wife went home to be with Christ, having ably and loyally supported him in all his labours.

Returning to Ireland in 1957, he remarried; his second wife being a native of Sion Mills, County Tyrone. While nursing in Londonderry she was brought into touch with assembly teaching, and despite her strong protestations that her position was scriptural, God's Word convinced her of the truth of baptism and showed her her place in assembly fellowship.

Having heard that there was no assembly in Dominica, they paid a visit there to 'spy out the land'. One cannot help but admire the vision and courage of these noble missionaries, who, obeying the word of their Master, would 'look on the fields'. Seeing possibilities and 'assuredly gathering' it was the mind of the Lord, they settled in Dominica in 1959, after a brief return visit to gather up their belongings, with the sympathy, prayers and support of the believers. As he plodded from house to house and village to village, his deep longing was for a time when, in this Roman Catholic stronghold, God would place His name.

In 1961 in the village of Salisbury, a large village on the west coast, God wrought in salvation and an assembly was formed. In 1962 a hall was built, and such was the progress of the work and the blessing of God, it soon became too small and a much larger building was erected. From those early, small beginnings when faint hearts might have given up, there are now five assemblies in the island with good Sunday schools and gospel activities.

In 1963, due to failing health, Mr McCune returned for a brief visit to Ireland. During his time at home he gave interesting accounts of what God had wrought as well as ministering in various parts. Feeling stronger in 1965, he left Belfast to return to Dominica. On the way he called to see a missionary couple, formerly of Barbados, and while in their home in Bristol, he took ill and was suddenly called to higher service. His remains were brought back to Belfast for burial at Whitechurch Cemetery, not far from his birth place at Cardy; Mr S. Jardine and Mr W. Bunting conducted the funeral services. There was a sense of joy at the funeral—a life lived for God and without blemish; yet a sense of loss—another noble warrior gone and where are the young men to fill up the ranks?

DR GEORGE McDONALD
1903-1981

Dr McDonald was saved when he was eight years of age, during the course of a serious illness, when he heard the doctor say there was no hope of recovery. He was quite young when he was received into the assembly at Bray. He gained the confidence and respect of the assembly, by his consistent life and keen interest in spiritual things. When he was ten years old, he believed God wanted him to serve in Africa and he purposed to go there if God guided and helped him. While studying for his medical degree, he kept things in a proper balance and consistently engaged in assembly matters. He helped in open-air meetings, which were quite a feature in the Dublin area in earlier years.

In 1928, he was married to Miss Eileen Young, who was then living in Dublin, and whose parents came from Scotland. In 1930, he was heartily commended to the work of the Lord, by the assemblies in Bray and Merrion Hall, Dublin. For many years missionary work was of great interest to the saints in Merrion Hall and they were happy to add another young couple to their list of missionaries.

They went first to Kabumbulu on the Lualaba river, Katanga province (now Shaba) and joined Dr Hoyte. It was a period of language learning and giving some medical assistance. He soon got a grasp of the Kilnba language and was eager to make known the gospel to those who spoke it. In 1931, he moved to Kidia, later going on to Masamba in North Katanga, to commence pioneer missionary work in an entirely new field. This involved clearing the forest, and building houses and places to accommodate medical work.

After some time of patient sowing of the good seed, fruit was seen and an assembly was formed and a hall erected. The gospel going out from that assembly, coupled with patients returning from getting medical care, resulted in the formation of twenty-six assemblies in the villages to the north of the mission station. Dr McDonald and his wife were indefatigable in their service; every opportunity and opening was made use of to reach out and see people saved.

When he left Africa and came back to reside in Dublin in 1958, his zeal was evident. He whole-heartedly gave himself to the making known of the gospel in Eire. He encouraged radio work, a new feature for gospel work in Ireland. By open-air work, Scripture distribution and getting groups of exercised young men to spread the gospel, he contributed much to the work of the Lord in the closing years of his life.

After a period of ill health, he died on 22nd April, 1981 in Sir Patrick Dunn's Hospital, Dublin, having spent his long life in devoted service to his Lord and Master. The well-attended funeral service was from Merrion Hall, where he often preached and sought to stir the saints regarding the furtherance of the gospel. His life-long friends Mr T.E.J. Archer and Mr H. Senior conducted the services.

MR W.C. McKEE

1897-1934

Mr McKee was born in February, 1897, the only son of a family of five. As a child he attended the Sunday school in Victoria Memorial Hall, one of the early assemblies in Belfast. He was saved when quite young and, being of a serious disposition, he took a real interest in spiritual matters. He took an active interest in gospel outreach, conducting gospel efforts in Ballywalter and other districts, and had God's seal of approval in blessing.

In 1920 he was commended to the work of the Lord in China; one of the first members of that assembly to be commended to missionary work. He went by ship via Australia, and the journey took three months. In a letter home he said, "When they build the Channel tunnel, one will be able to go by train from England to Peking". If his mail was properly addressed 'via Siberia', it took a month. He wrote how a letter home to Belfast travelled—"First, the postmen carry the letters, travelling in relays day and night, walking or riding on donkeys the three hundred miles to Peking, then on by train to Manchuria, across Siberia, past lake Baikal to Moscow, then to Poland and Berlin, to Ostend and by ship to England".

He lived in primitive conditions and his letters home showed how much he was dependent upon his sisters and others for even the very small things of life. He asked for these to be sent with his letters, as parcels by sea would take so long. He mentioned, "a decent lead pencil, burners for my paraffin lamp, a hacksaw blade, black cotton socks, bandages and three sheets of fine sandpaper". He said, "It is

intensely cold and can be lonely; if friends at home knew what it is to be away from their loved ones, I think they would write oftener". Many beloved missionaries still feel like this.

Writing home in 1931, he said, "I have bought two goats, a cow and a calf, so we should have plenty of milk, cream and butter". Much of his period of service was spent living alone. He became engaged to a nurse from Australia, Miss Mary E. Jennings, and was looking forward to going there to be married, but God willed it otherwise. Her letters after his death showed her resignation to the will of God, and her continued desire to serve the Lord in the sphere He would choose.

He started Sunday schools, visited hundreds of villages giving out tracts and preaching in the open-air, very many Bibles and christian calendars were left in the hands of these poor dark people; only eternity will reveal the harvest. He laboured a lot alone, and at other times with brethren of like mind, namely, Messrs McColm, Duthie and Witheridge. Although his period of service was short, he put much into it for God. He had surgery in 1934, and after that contracted smallpox, of which there was quite an epidemic at that time. He was taken to the house of Mr and Mrs Witheridge, as Mrs Witheridge was a fully-qualified nurse. She did all in her power to save his life, but was not able. It is interesting to note that she had known his fiancée; they nursed together in a Brisbane hospital. When he passed away early in the morning, Mr Witheridge phoned Mr Duthie, and together they arranged his funeral. A Chinese brother read 1st Thessalonians 4:13-18, giving words of comfort and gospel truth. Mr Duthie spoke at the grave, after which a hymn was sung in Chinese.

MR GERALD B. McQUILLAN
1910-1971

Mr McQuillan was born in London into a Roman Catholic home. Early in life he was brought to Malin, County Donegal, where he was brought up, spending his youthful days in the pleasures and frivolities of the district.

One day while working with a farmer and ploughing, a group of visitors from Northern Ireland asked if they could take a picture of him with the plough and horses. After taking the picture, one, a Mr W.W. Lewis, said he would like to sing a hymn, which he did. In later life, Gerald would have said that it was the first little bit of gospel to reach his heart:

> "Nothing in my hand I bring;
> Simply to Thy cross I cling;
> Naked, come to Thee for dress;
> Helpless, look to Thee for grace;
> Foul, I to the fountain fly—
> Wash me, Saviour, or I die."

In the year 1935 he went to work in Craigavad, County Down and got lodgings in a christian home. The atmosphere in that home made deep impressions on him and soon his spiritual need gave him real concern. Coming home from chapel his attention was arrested by a large text, John 3:16, painted on a hayshed near Bangor. He attended some gospel meetings conducted by the late Mr F. Bingham, and God used John 3:16 to bring him into the

knowledge of salvation. Soon he was baptised and received into Central Hall assembly, Bangor.

The change in his life and conduct was very marked and spiritual life was manifested in his behaviour. Soon after being saved, he went to visit in the home of Mrs Starret at Priestfield, County Donegal. A Roman Catholic man employed there who knew him in earlier days was asked, after a meal with him, what he thought of Gerald now. He said, "If he is as well changed inside as he is outside, he will do!" In later years that dear man himself got saved.

In 1942 he was married to Miss M. Lammie of the assembly at Fintona, County Tyrone. His interest in the gospel was seen in his increasing activity in Sunday school work, tract distribution and gospel preaching, but God was burdening his heart about wider and needy fields. In 1946, the assembly was happy to commend him to the grace of God for work in Rhodesia (now Zambia).

Mr J. Geddis had spent some time in Northern Ireland giving reports of the work and the great need in Northern Rhodesia. Gerald, with a number of others, believing God was calling them, responded and in 1946 left the homelands to carry the gospel to others in darkness, as he had once been. He laboured first with Mr Geddis and while learning the Lunda language, gave help in building halls and homes; not an easy task in extreme heat and working with hard timbers.

When knowing enough of the language to be able to make known the gospel, he laboured assiduously in Sunday school work, prison visitation and ministering to the sick in hospital. After Sunday school on Lord's Days, he preached in the hospital wards and sang hymns, his sonorous voice echoing through the building. Village preaching in the evenings by a large fire, which burned to warn off mosquitoes, proved fruitful. When there was trouble in Angola, a large refugee camp was established a few miles from Zambeze and there a good gospel work was done.

Mrs McQuillan was called to be with the Lord in March, 1951, and Mr McQuillan returned to Ireland with his two small children. In December, 1952 he married Miss Sarah Armour, who was then in fellowship in Kingsbridge assembly, Belfast. Returning to Africa he again threw himself into the work and is remembered by fellow missionaries as a zealous hard-working brother.

In June, 1971, he took the Stewart family to the Copperbelt on the first stage of their trip home on furlough. On the return journey, he and his son Samuel were involved in a motor accident. They collided with a large mine truck carrying copper ore which was hidden in a dust cloud, and was in the process of overtaking another vehicle. Gerald was killed instantly, but an African driver found Samuel unconscious and took him seventy miles to the nearest hospital, where he recovered from multiple injuries.

Gerald's funeral was conducted by Messrs Halliday, Croudace, and Geddis, with some of his beloved African brethren sharing in the service, which was held in Zambezi Gospel Hall. In a little bush cemetery outside Zambezi a plaque, mounted on a concrete slab, marks the grave. His name, age, date of conversion, etc., are written on the plaque, as well as a verse in Lunda "Akufwa Mudi Yesu Anakooleki", Rev. 14:13.

God granted him his desire, "to spend and be spent" in the land to which he was called. His widow and family returned and settled in Ireland.

We marvel at the wisdom and grace of God, bringing a Roman Catholic youth from County Donegal, saving him in County Down, and sending him to Africa, where he was made a blessing to many. We can only say with Paul, "O the depth of the riches both of the wisdom and knowledge of God! how unsearchable are his judgments, and his ways past finding out!", Rom. 11:33.

MR TOM REA

1890-1980

Mr Rea was born in Lurgan, Northern Ireland on 7th April, 1890. Being brought up in a godly home, he was made aware of his need of a Saviour and in early life he was saved. From the beginning of his christian life he actively interested himself in gospel work in the villages and towns around, while at the same time carefully studying the Scriptures. He was a keen student right to the end of life.

In 1911 he was commended to the work of the Lord in Africa, by Victoria Hall and Ormeau Road assemblies in Belfast; later Holborn Hall assembly, Bangor, joined in this. He accompanied Mr and Mrs Hugh Cunningham, who at that time were labouring at Kalunda in Angola. The journey took seventy-one days, much of it on foot. Those were pioneering days when the only means of transport was by barge, with native paddlers, on the rivers in the interior, and walking single file on the nine-inch paths through the forests, travelling fifteen to twenty miles a day, with African carriers carrying sixty pound loads. Mail was slow and uncertain. Their homes were built of mud and wattle with grass roofs and dirt floors. There was no modern plumbing. The mattresses on their home-made beds were calico sacks filled with corn husks and their food was mostly native produced.

His first five or six years at Kalunda were spent in getting a thorough knowledge of the Lunda language and doing pioneer work in the villages. He came home on his first furlough in 1917 and on his return to Kalunda met Miss Ethel Isherwood, from Manchester, England, who

during his absence had joined the Cunninghams in their work. In 1918 he and Miss Isherwood were married at Kalene Hill Mission. In 1923, when the Cunninghams moved from Angola to Northern Rhodesia, (now Zambia), the Reas went to the Belgian Congo, (now Zaire). Along with Mr Jack Prescott they pioneered a new work at Tshiwilu. Brethren in the homelands had provided Mr Rea with a printing press which, to move, took one hundred men! First at Kalunda and later in the Congo he did a lot of printing of the various books of the New Testament as they were translated.

After three years at Tshiwilu they were ordered to move by the Belgian authorities who thought they were too near the Rhodesian border. They then moved to a new site at Nyama where he concentrated mainly on the translation of the Bible (in collaboration with Mr Singleton Fisher). In thinking of those days his son Eric says, "I can remember clearly his being locked up for hours each day with Manase and one or two others in that painstaking work".

Mr Rea was an accomplished linguist, speaking French, Lunda, Zovale and, in later years, Chokwe. He was an expert in Lunda and, along with his dear friends and fellow-workers, Mr and Mrs Singleton Fisher, translated and revised the whole Bible as well as many hymns and other literature into that language.

After three years at Nyanama, Mr and Mrs Rea went to Muchacha and then to Dilolo on the Congo-Angola border, where Mr Rea had some of the happiest and most fruitful years of his life amongst the Chokwe people whom he greatly loved. Mrs Rea was also much used and blessed there among the women and children. During those years Mr Rea made several extended visits to Angola and his rich expository ministry, both in the Chokwe language and in English, interpreted into Umbundu, will be long remembered by the missionaries and the African believers. In 1942 they returned to Belfast and at the end of World War II, they returned to Zambia. Later, when Mrs Rea's health deteriorated, they spent two years in Cape Town, where Mr Rea's ministry was greatly appreciated; then they came back to Ireland, via USA, at which time Mrs Rea died.

In 1968 he married Mrs Johnston, who devotedly gave him twelve years of great care and happiness. He greatly enjoyed moving amongst the assemblies and the homes of the believers. He was loved and respected and his ministry was conducive to godliness and spiritual prosperity, making deep and lasting impressions upon many.

His physical strength and his mind remained active and alert until his home-call in his 91st year. After a few days illness he was taken home to his well-earned rest and reward, without a stain or blemish on his record as a servant of God. He died on 1st May, 1980, and his wife passed away five years later. His funeral was from Castlereagh Gospel Hall. That large hall was packed to overflowing as the saints gathered to pay tribute to one of Ireland's great sons. Messrs Wishart, Hutchinson and Aiken were responsible for the funeral services. The burial was at Roselawn Cemetery, Belfast.

In reviewing his life in Africa we see that his main contribution is, first, his translation of the Bible into Lunda, a monumental task, and then, his gift of training African leaders among young men, with whom he had a very special relationship. These men have stood the test of time and have been used of God in founding and building up numerous assemblies in Angola, Zaire, and Zambia. The "record is on high"; the final appraisement will be made clear on "that day".

Mr Rea was a typical Ulster christian gentleman, of good appearance and quick step. He could at times be blunt with a mixture of Irish humour and quick repartee. He was a man of strict integrity who had no time for hypocrisy or pious humbug. He ordered his life as before God, one hundred percent true to God and His Word, and loyal to the core to the Person of Christ. We could well say, "whose faith follow".

MR JOHN RUDDOCK
1897-1988

Mr Ruddock was born at Growell, Co. Down, on 17th December, 1897, the son of Andrew Ruddock, the Evangelist. He was saved at the age of 21 while working on an electric plant. Deeply concerned about spiritual matters, on 26th September, 1918, he fell on his knees and cried aloud, "God be merciful to me a sinner". Almost immediately he began his life of service by joining Mr T.E. Wilson (later missionary in Africa) to give out tracts and preach in the open-air.

In 1921, due to his father's health, the entire Ruddock family went to the U.S.A. locating in Los Angeles. In the Mexican district of Los Angeles, John commenced a gospel work which led to the formation of an assembly, which is still thriving. At that time he was exercised to go to Mexico, but it was then closed to missionaries. In 1926 he married Miss Janet R. Baird, who came from Kilwinning, Scotland, and God blessed the union with two daughters.

In October, 1926 they were commended by the Jefferson Gospel Hall Assembly to the work of the Lord in Guatemala, Central America. For some time they lived in Quetzaltenango, later moving to San Felipe, Guatemala. In 1931 they moved to Honduras where there was only one missionary couple, Mr and Mrs Alfred Hockings from England, and the need was very great. Honduras was, and still is, the poorest and most backward of the Central American countries. For many years the Hockings and Ruddocks were the only missionaries in the Northern part of this country.

John and his wife spent the first year with the Hockings
in San Pedro Sula, then they located in Trujillo, where
there was no gospel work of any kind. For four years they
laboured and encountered bitter opposition; then fruit
began to appear, at first amongst the Caribs, and several
assemblies were formed. In 1942 they moved to Tela,
where they lived until 1978, when age and increasing
weakness caused them to leave and reside in California.

When they first joined the work in Honduras, there was
only one assembly in the country—today there are well
nigh 200. The Ruddocks were appreciated and loved by
thousands of believers all over the Republic of Honduras.
Only God knows how much this noble couple contributed
to the work of God in Central America during fifty-two
years of dedicated service. The gospel was preached, saints
were taught, assemblies formed and halls erected. The
means of travel were limited; they rode on mules and many
long journeys were undertaken on foot. They pioneered
into remote parts and saw the work of God prospering.
Despite frequent attacks of malaria and primitive conditions
they laboured diligently.

He had a care for elderly saints and had a home built for
them in Tela. He designed it in its entirety and did much of
the building with his own hands. The Mayor of Tela
speaking of it said, "Speaking of the many works which
have been accomplished, the most extraordinary is the old
people's home—those who are fortunate enough to live in
this home live a life of leisure and comfort, everything is
provided; shelter, food, clothing and medical attention. It is
the work of a married couple, John and Nettie Ruddock,
They did a good work in Trujillo, they then settled in Tela. I
want to take this opportunity of advising the people of Tela
about this work. If there is anything that should be
recognised in Tela, it is that this work, in truth, is a
wonderful asset to the city". How nice to have 'a good
report of them that are without'. The animosity toward
them and their gospel efforts, in part fomented and
encouraged by the Roman Catholic priests, had disappeared
and they were admired and respected by all.

Over the years others joined them and together they

laboured harmoniously with Mr and Mrs A. Sheddon, Mr and Mrs S. Hanna, Mr and Mrs W. Tidsbury, Mr and Mrs S. Hanlon and A. Hockings. In 1978 they went to reside in Western Assemblies Home in Claremont, California, where on 21st February, 1988, he died peacefully in his sleep. A short time before his decease he sent the following poem to a missionary magazine in U.S.A.

If you had been to foreign lands,
Where weary souls stretch out their hands
To plead, yet no one understands;
Would you go back? Would you?

If you had seen the women bear
Their heavy loads with none to share;
Had heard them weep, with none to care;
Would you go back? Would you?

If you had seen them in despair,
Beat their breasts, and pull their hair,
While demon powers filled the air;
Would you go back? Would you?

If you had walked through Honduras sand,
Your hand within the Saviour's hand
And knew He'd called you to that land;
Would you go back? Would you?

If you had seen the Christian die,
With ne'er a fear tho' death was nigh,
Had seen them smile and say goodbye,
Would you go back? Would you?

Yet still they wait, a weary throng,
They've waited, some so very long,
When shall despair be turned to song?
I'm going back! Would you?

Yes, I would go back. But no I can't,
I have gone back and back and back.
Now I've reached four score and ten,
My legs are stiff and painful too,
My eyes are dim, my hearing gone,
More fit for Heaven, than travelling now.
No, I can't go back. Can you? Can you?

The funeral service was conducted by Mr Don Thompson, assisted by Mr A. Sheddon and Mr Jorge Chimilio, a Carib Indian, representing the people of Honduras.

MR DREW THOMPSON
1905-1984

Mr Thompson was born in County Tyrone, a few miles from the market town of Omagh; his parents were devoted believers. From earliest days he was instructed in the Scriptures and knew the truths of the gospel. When he was almost 20 years old he was saved at meetings conducted by Mr Robert Hawthorne at Ardstraw, a village near Drew's home. From the very beginning he said his joy in salvation was so great that he talked to almost everyone he came in contact with.

His exercise concerning the spread of the gospel was very definite. He taught in the Sunday school and helped in open-air meetings which used to take place very frequently in many parts of Ulster. He also shared in series of nightly meetings with like-minded brethren. Mr W. Rogers, that capable Bible teacher, was a regular visitor to the Ardstraw assembly and his teaching helped to guide Drew and build his christian character.

It was something Mr Hawthorne said to him that first created exercise regarding the work of the Lord abroad. He considered Venezuela, but his way was not clear in that direction and God guided him toward Uruguay. For eleven years he prayed and waited before God for definite tokens of Divine leading. Finally, deciding it was God's path for him, his brethren in Ardstraw, joined by the assemblies in Kilmore and Sion Mills, commended him to the grace of God. At that time the promise of God was real to him— "My presence shall go with thee and I will give thee rest". After his death, his wife said, "Despite difficulties and trials

for forty-nine years we have enjoyed that rest".

In November, 1935 he was married to Miss Margaret Crowe, and on 13th January, 1936 they sailed for Uruguay. They came home on furlough in 1948, 1960, 1967, and lastly in 1974. He was not the eloquent type of preacher, nor did he have the strong personality of others mentioned in this book, but he was an earnest, conscientious, God-fearing brother, who laboured for almost half a century in Uruguay. God rewarded his faithful labours in souls being saved and God's people being guided in Divine ways. Some in whom he took an interest have been saved since he was taken home.

He distributed thousands of tracts and constantly preached in the open-air. The summer before his death was spent almost every evening in open-air witness—if others were free they helped him, if not, he stood alone. Small assemblies and isolated believers were a burden to him and he travelled extensively in seeking to help them. Mr H.W. Graham and Mr R. Adamson were from time to time his fellow-labourers.

While visiting a married daughter and some friends he was stricken with a severe stroke, and for two weeks he was critically ill in the British hospital in Montevideo. When that crisis passed he was taken to his other daughter's home, where for nine months, with the help of a doctor friend of the family, and the Lord's sustaining grace, he was tenderly cared for. During all this time of illness he was happy and enjoyed the Lord's presence, spending much time in prayerful intercession for Uruguay and its great spiritual need.

On the 26th May, 1984, he passed into the presence of his Lord and Master. A local evangelist and a business man conducted the funeral services, paying brief tribute to Drew and giving solemn gospel messages. His body was interred in the local British cemetery. His widow and two daughters remained in Uruguay.

MR H.B. THOMPSON
Went home in 1926

Hugh B. Thompson was born in the city of Armagh, Northern Ireland. His parents were christians, members of the Church of Ireland, and they taught their children their need of being born again. It was on the 14th October, 1877, at the seaside home of his parents in Rostrevor that he was brought to the Lord through reading a tract in which the words appeared, "Behold I stand at the door and knock." This spoke to his heart, and as a result he opened the door, accepted Christ as his Saviour and Lord and was truly saved. A little time later he was baptized and associated himself with an assembly of believers meeting in the Lord's Name in Armagh. From the beginning of his christian life he witnessed for Christ in the towns and villages near his home. In 1885 in company with a band of young men he spent his summer holidays in the north of England preaching the Gospel and visiting in the homes of the people. This he regarded as an excellent training school for what lay ahead in Central Africa.

In 1881 Mr Fred. Stanley Arnot, a young man of 21 years of age, left Scotland for Africa following in the footsteps of David Livingstone. Landing at Durban in East Africa and travelling by ox-wagon and often on foot he made his way into the interior, first in Barotseland, then in Garenganze, where the notorious chief Msidi had his capital. From there he proceeded west to Portuguese Angola where he arrived in 1886. On all these pioneer journeys he endured incredible hardships. After seven years, in September 1888, he returned to Britain.

108

His reports among the assemblies of the need in Central Africa caused widespread interest. A number of devoted men and women volunteered to accompany him when he returned to Africa in March, 1889. Among them were two men from Northern Ireland, Mr Robert Johnston, a devoted evangelist, and Mr H.B. Thompson. One tragedy after another overtook the party and Mr Johnston died of fever just as the ship was arriving at Benguela on the west coast of Africa and he was buried in the Roman Catholic cemetery there. The christians in Northern Ireland sent out a tombstone with John 3:16 inscribed on it in the Portuguese language, to mark the spot. The survivors of the party pushed on into the interior, but at Bailundu, 200 miles from the coast, two other members of the missionary party, Messrs Morris and Gall, died one night of malaria. After another 100 miles, at Kuanjululu, Mr Joseph Lynn was bitten by a mad dog and died of rabies.

Three years previously, Mr C.A. Swan from England and Mr William Faulkner from Canada had penetrated Garenganze to Msidi's capital to relieve Mr Arnot. They had been alone during this time and had witnessed terrible scenes of murder and bloodshed perpetrated by the tyrant chief. Three members of the party brought out by Mr Arnot, volunteered to go ahead to relieve Messrs Swan and Faulkner in Garenganze and bring with them needed supplies. The three volunteers were Messrs F.T. Lane, Dan Crawford, and H.B. Thompson—an Englishman, a Scot and an Irishman. The journey of approximately 1,000 miles had to be undertaken on foot with African porters carrying the supplies. On arrival at Msidi's capital they found a Belgian expedition of soldiers, commanded by two English officers, Captain Stairs and Captain Bodson, who had been commissioned by the King of the Belgians to take over the country for Belgium. The missionaries were asked to withdraw outside the capital while negotiations were taking place. Captain Stairs had his headquarters on a hill outside Msidi's compound where they proposed to hoist the Belgian flag. Captain Bodson, his second-in-command, with some African soldiers entered Msidi's compound and demanded that the chief come out and be present at the ceremony of raising the flag. Msidi pled for time to consult with his councillors. This led to a heated argument. Msidi remarked, "This sounds like war and not peace," and spat on the ground. Bodson took this as an insult, and drawing his pistol, fired and shot Msidi in the chest. The chief staggered into his house and immediately expired. One of Msidi's body-guards, Musaka, lifted his gun, fired, and shot Bodson, who fell instantly and died. Captain Stairs ordered the bodies of Msidi and Bodson to be taken to his camp. There they beheaded the chief and the headless body was buried some two hundred yards from where he was shot. From that moment the great tyrant Msidi, whose terrible deeds had stricken terror into thousands for hundreds of miles—north, south, east, and west—was stripped of his power. After his death the population scattered in fear, but the missionaries gathered them together and settled the country. The native greeting and slogan became "Mutende" (peace). Previous to Msidi's death, Mr Swan had left on his first furlough for the west coast and England in the company of a Belgian officer, Lieutenant Le Marinel. Mr Faulkner, who had been with Mr Swan for three years, had been seriously ill most of that time and had been tenderly cared for by his fellow missionary Mr Swan. Mr Thompson offered to escort Mr Faulkner on the difficult and dangerous journey to the coast, on his way home to Canada. On his arrival back in Garenganze, after Msidi's death, Mr Thompson joined Mr Dan Crawford in a move to Lake Mweru where a new centre was founded at Luanza. Mr Benjamin Cobbe from Northern Ireland who had come in from the east coast with Mr Arnot joined them later, but tragically died within a year. Crawford and Thompson were both individualists and pioneers. Crawford evangelised in the north-east and south and Thompson in the north-west. On one of these pioneer trips Mr Thompson suffered a severe injury to one of his eyes and, after seven years in Africa, where he witnessed many of the above historical events which changed the map of the so-called dark continent, he gave the rest of his life to preaching the Gospel and ministering the Word in Britain.

H.B. Thompson was a dignified, courteous, christian

gentleman. He spoke with a very wide vocabulary of beautiful English. He was a careful student of the Scriptures with very strong convictions about vital doctrines. Mr C.A. Swan said that while others were off hunting or engaging in chores around the camp, Mr Thompson would be sitting under a tree studying his Newberry Bible. It was characteristic of the man. He passed away at Bangor, County Down on 25th November, 1926. "Whose faith follow."

MR JOSEPH W. TURKINGTON

1918-1982

Mr Turkington was born on 28th December, 1918 in Lurgan; his parents were saved people. His father died while quite a young man, and his mother, a godly woman, raised her six children, often with much self-sacrifice. When Joe was 10 years old he got saved and for a number of years was in fellowship with Baptists. He came in contact with Mr John McCann, who later went to serve the Lord in Brazil, while working in a linen factory. John endeavoured to show him New Testament church truth, and when Joe would contend for his position, John would say, "Well Joe, just keep on reading your Bible." This he did and later, as a result of personal conviction, he sought fellowship in the Lurgan assembly.

He showed real interest in all the affairs of the assembly—"was with them coming in and going out." He took part in gospel work amongst young and old, and while engaged in secular work, he conducted spells of nightly meetings. God set the seal of His approval on the work in the salvation of souls. It will be noticed by the reader, how that men who turned out to be successful missionaries in foreign fields, were missonaries at home. At times when it is made known that some are seeking commendation, the saints are surprised, there being no sign of previous prosperity in gospel work.

In 1947, he was commended by the Lurgan assembly and on the last day of that year he left for his field of service. The first two years were spent with Mr J.E. Fairfield, in learning the language and getting to know the people. In

1949, he married Miss Ruth Saword, a daughter of Mr S.J. Saword, who was a veteran missionary, and together they made their first home in San Carlos. It was small and humble, and they sought with personal sacrifice to take the gospel to that needy state. Only God knows the sacrifice and privations as they encountered primitive conditions, bad roads and the problem of getting to isolated places. All would have combined to discourage, but our brother, loyally supported by his wife, was zealous and tireless in his labours. God worked, souls were saved and assemblies were formed.

He shared in gospel work with Mr Saword and other brethren. Some of the results of these labours are seen in the four assemblies in the state of Cojedes, two in the adjoining state of Portuguesa, and another in Apure. The work in the latter place was one that called for patience and endurance, due to long journeys, long periods away from home and much sectarian confusion. He travelled extensively, preaching, teaching, and erecting halls. He was a diligent worker who spared neither mind nor muscle in God's work. God gave him seven sons, who are all saved and show much interest in Divine matters, and give valuable help in areas where their father spent his life.

Due to heart trouble he returned to Ireland for surgery. While awaiting this he kept busy and was esteemed by the christians—his happy smile and pleasant personality endeared him to all. It was a great shock when he failed to survive the operation, and went to be with the Lord on 11th July, 1982. The very large funeral was from Lurgan Gospel Hall. Mr J. Walmsley, a fellow missionary, flew from Canada to share in the service. Mr A. McShane and Mr Walmsley spoke in the hall, paying eloquent tribute to a beloved brother. Mr S. Ferguson gave the message at the graveside, with Messrs J. Wells and J. Thompson sharing in prayer. Thus was laid to rest the remains of another who gave his life "for My sake and the gospel's."

MR CHARLES T. WRIGHT

Mr Wright was in army service and was sent to India in 1894. After almost two years there he was saved. He worked nine months after conversion in a soldiers' home at Coonor. Leaving that he went to Darjeeling to work in the gospel amongst the Tibetans, where he spent a year. He then spent some time amongst the Moravians. God blessed His Word in salvation. In 1903 he returned to the U.K. and took charge of a soldiers' home in Limerick. Knowing something of the loneliness and many temptations of army life, he had a compassion for the soldiers and tried to be of spiritual help.

In 1904 he returned to the work on the Tibetan border, accompanied by Mr T. Taylor, later moving over to Ghoom near Darjeeling. In 1905 he married Miss M. Elizabeth Ogden from England. After eight years of pioneering work he returned to the U.K. In 1915 they returned to India and after a period of itinerant service he settled in the Dagshai district. In 1917 an Indian brother joined in the work and together they "laboured much" in the gospel.

He had deep interest in the Tibetan people and in 1921 and 1922 paid extended visits to the borders of that dark and needy land. Only eternity will reveal the results of that patient sowing of the good seed. In 1923 he had a further furlough and spent almost a year seeking to arouse interest in those needy fields. Returning in 1924, to again visit the Tibetan border areas, they laboured diligently for a further six years. 1930 saw another brief visit to the U.K. and, when he returned, he remained in India until finally leaving in 1935 to finish his life in the U.K. The remaining years of life were spent in intercession for those he had seen saved and for the many places he was concerned about but unable to reach with the gospel. It was in his heart to do it. 1 Kings 8:17-18.

MR R.J. WRIGHT
1906-1988

Mr Wright was born in Strabane on 5th September, 1906. He was the eldest son of Mr S. Wright, an earnest and esteemed evangelist, who was widely used of God in Ireland. He was saved on 18th January, 1918; God used Mr John Blair, an Irish evangelist who travelled widely in making known the gospel, in his conversion. Bobbie, as he was known, was received into the Strabane assembly. In 1928 he qualified as a chemist. Being brought up in a home where evangelists and missionaries often met, he became interested in the Lord's work, especially in foreign lands. This interest deepened and was with him to the closing hours of life. Learning of Japan with its ninety million people, most of whom had never heard the gospel, he left Ireland in 1931. He found employment as a chemist with C.B.K. Argall in Kobe, whose thriving pharmaceutical business attracted a clientele of fairly wealthy American, German and British executives. He lodged with the Argalls, who were English speaking, so his progress with the Japanese language was virtually nil. After two years he gave up his job and comfortable lodgings to rent a small room and enrol for language classes. After some time he moved to Tokyo where he, Dr Tsukiyana and Fujimoto preached the gospel every night.

Assembly matters recalled him to Kobe, where appalling living conditions, lack of proper meals, and an inevitable sense of alienation took a heavy physical and emotional toll, causing his return to Ireland in 1937. Despite his weakened condition he came across Russia and Siberia by

train, to see what possibilities there were for gospel work. A year later he returned to Japan accompanied by Mr John Hewitt, who later died in a concentration camp, and has been described by some as 'the first protestant martyr in Japan'.

He continued to reach out with the gospel and was privileged to see God working. In 1941, war-time conditions brought all foreigners under suspicion. He and John Hewitt were closely questioned and had to leave the country. He was put on the Tatsuda Maru for U.S.A., but the journey had scarce begun when Pearl Harbour was bombed by the Japanese. The ship returned to Japan and Bobbie was interned in poor conditions for eight months before being repatriated. When being interrogated he was faced with the following: "If this Jesus you preach is coming back to reign on earth and all will have to bow and acknowledge His supreme Lordship, that will mean even our Emperor will have to do this". They then said, "To bow to one greater than our Emperor would be treason". Had they been Japanese citizens, in all likelihood they would have been executed immediately. He was freed in October 1942, when he returned to Ireland. In 1943, he worked as locum for chemists in Larne and Carrickfergus. In August 1945, he married Miss Eirene Edgar BSc. God blessed the union with six children. In 1948 they settled in Tokyo and continuing in gospel work they saw souls saved and assemblies formed. In 1931 there was one small assembly in Kobe, today there are over one hundred in Japan.

Bobbie was largely responsible for the formation of the Evangelical Publishing Depot, which to date has produced up to fifty million tracts in addition to christian magazines, booklets and hymn books. He engaged in prison visitation and was granted permission to visit all Japanese prisons. When a severe back injury forced him to leave Japan in 1960, he was honoured for his work by the Minister of Justice, who presented him with an illuminated address and a silver cup. He was the first foreigner to be so recognised. But what pleased him best was, he was given ten minutes to preach the gospel on closed circuit television and the message was beamed to every prison cell in Japan.

On returning to Ireland he went back into the pharmaceutical business, but, as the work of the gospel was uppermost in his mind, he simply used his business to pay expenses and help others. He visited the prisons in Ulster and was responsible for a gospel work at Whitehead, where a nice building has been erected and some forty christians are in fellowship.

He was a unique man, often very unorthodox, but a happy likeable man, who had a mischievous twinkle in his eye. Few had his continuous zeal and enthusiasm. He may at times have used the most unusual prayers, poems and practices, (as the letter published will show), but his motive was always right. His passion for the souls of men controlled his life until, on 3rd May, 1988, he was called to be with the Lord.

His very large funeral was the first to be from the new hall at Whitehead. Messrs Wishart, Farrell, Andrews and Hall shared the services in the hall and at the graveside.

C/o Messrs Carpus & Alexander
Catering Agents
Ephesus & Troas
20/2/1949

Beloved Brethren

With reference to your invitation to come over the border into Macedonia and help there, I was rather surprised at your apparent expectancy, and scant information. I cannot say anything at the present, "until the way opens up" as I have been exercised about Antioch and needy villages near Jerusalem. In the meantime, send me the following information:

First of all, is Macedonia evangelized or not; have they our Jewish religion or are they heathen? This is important as I cannot afford to waste my time and talent on unopened districts, and we can't reach the heathen with our Gospel. How many assemblies are there?

While it is true that I live by faith, my car will only go on petrol, and with changed conditions you can no longer expect men, especially with a family, to rush into new fields with no other information than a call of need, and I am now much too practical to be influenced by a dream. What accommodation facilities exist? Who are the influential brethren?

I am glad to say that the old-fashioned, vulgar type of baggy-kneed house-canvasser preacher has disappeared. The Gospel demands the dignity of a black bag and umbrella. I do not visit widows' houses or make long prayers at home, and am so separated that I only visit influential christians' homes, especially on meal invitations.

I have a special Conference ministry gift and can easily hold the platform for half an hour or more, and... incidentally... supplement my gifts. Quite frequently I confine myself to taking local Sunday services in Gospel halls to discourage local amateurish gift, and encourage other gifts (£1 per night in Asia). I still carry on my tent work, though I no longer make tents and confine this work to the neighbourhood of Gospel Halls, as ceilings are too low to permit erection inside.

I preach nothing heterodox. The whole "truth" with special emphasis on our being seated with Christ in Heavenly places, and silence on adventurous activity in earthly places. I only use the small book of Acts for texts.

I will appreciate a speedy reply as I am at Laodicea for the Bible readings on the seven churches. "Some interest, saints cheered", and hope to "be at Jerusalem" for Easter where I will speak on "Types and Shadows".

Sincerely yours,
Saul of Tarsus.

God's Call To Special Service

T.Ernest Wilson
(Abridged by kind permission)

To many of God's people a definite individual call to service is a mystery. They think that the presentation of a need constitutes in itself a call to meet that need, and there is no necessity for anything further. Others would say that the general call of the Great Commission to go into all the world and preach the Gospel of Matthew 28 and Mark 16 is all that is needed for one to embark on a lifetime of missionary work in the great harvest field. This may sound plausible, but reasoning of this kind has resulted in many a tragedy. Some run unsent and fall out by the way and as a result become bitter and cynical.

The Bible speaks of at least three calls:

(1) **To Salvation, Matthew 11:28,29.** When obeyed it is an effectual calling.

(2) **To Sacrifice, Romans 12:1,2.** To consecration and discipleship.

(3) **To Service, Mark 1:17.** To become fishers of men.

Every believer has a fivefold relationship. He is:

a child in a family;
a member in a body;
a priest in a temple;
a citizen in a kingdom;
a servant in the harvest field.

In the sphere of service, it is incumbent for every Christian to find out from the Lord of the harvest what is the work which the Lord has fitted him or her to do. This means much time spent in prayer in the secret place with

122

God. The Sovereign Lord is the One who calls, prepares and sends the servant, and shows him the task he is to perform.

There are examples in the Bible, of men who were called by God to do a specific work. Their call is described in detail. Each one is different, but there are some features which are common to all. Each one had definite intimate dealings with God in the secret of His presence, when God spoke to his heart, called him and used him in His service.

The supreme example of a call to service, unique in every sense of the word, is our Lord Himself. "I the Lord have called Thee in righteousness, and will hold Thy hand, and will keep Thee and give Thee for a covenant of the people, for a light of the Gentiles; to open the blind eyes, to bring out the prisoners from the prison, and them that sit in darkness out of the prison house" Isaiah 42:6. He of course is the Perfect Servant of Jehovah, and His work is so beautifully described in Isaiah 40-66.

A study of these men will show that they were human like ourselves, with many weaknesses and failures, and yet God used them mightily in His service. The striking thing about each one is that they were individually called by God to do a specific work and were fitted for it and sustained in it.

The Call of ABRAHAM

The call of Abraham was a watershed in human history. According to Usher's chronology, he lived exactly half way between Adam and Christ. The first eleven chapters of Genesis cover approximately two thousand years, and from Genesis 12 to the Incarnation covers the same period of time. The dispensations of conscience and human government are coming to an end and God is about to do something new. "The God of Glory appeared unto our father Abraham when he was in Mesopotamia before he dwelt in Charran and said unto him, Get thee out of thy country, and from thy kindred, and come into the land which I shall show thee" Acts 7:1-3. Ur of the Chaldees at that time was a highly developed civilisation, as Sir Leonard Wooley the archaeologist discovered in 1926. We are told that Abraham was wealthy. He was very rich in cattle, in silver and in gold, Genesis 13:2. To obey God and leave the sophisticated environment of Ur and go to Canaan was like leaving Park Avenue in New York and going to Timbuktoo. And yet he obeyed the divine call and stepped out in simple faith on God's promise. But like many another pilgrim since, he ran into problems.

THE TESTS OF FAITH

The first problem came from his FAMILY. The Lord had called Abram but apparently his father Terah took over control of the emigrating party. "Terah took Abram his son, and Lot the son of Haran his son's son, and Sarai his daughter-in-law, his son Abram's wife; and they went forth with them from Ur of the Chaldees to go into the land
124

of Canaan; and they came unto Haran and dwelt there. And the days of Terah were 205 years and Terah died in Haran" Genesis 11:31,32. Haran was on the border between Mesopotamia and Canaan. The great river Euphrates separated the two countries. One can understand the feelings of Terah. To cross the river was a complete break with the old life and land, and he preferred to stop halfway. But he died! Abram was now free to act. The hindrance to complete obedience was now removed. Many today encounter this difficulty when they attempt to obey the call of God. "A man's foes shall be they of his own household. He that loveth father or mother more than Me is not worthy of Me" Matthew 10:36,37. Jonathan, David's beloved friend, was torn between loyalty to his father and love for David. He made his choice, went back to the camp of Saul and lost his life on the wrong side, 1 Samuel 20.

Abram's next test was FAMINE. He crossed the Euphrates and came into the land of promise. From that time on he was called the Hebrew—the man from across the river. That river separated him forever from Babylonia. He never took a furlough back to Ur. He remained a pilgrim and a stranger with an altar and a tent until the end. But there was a famine in the land. This can be a severe test in any age. More than 50% of the world's population goes to bed hungry every night. Even God's children can die of starvation as recent events in Angola have shown. There can be a famine in Bethlehem, the house of bread, and both Moab and Egypt can be attractive as places of retreat. But either one is dangerous ground as Elimelech and Abram discovered.

Abram decided to go down to Egypt where he encountered his next test, that of FEAR. He was afraid for his life on account of his beautiful wife Sarai. He asked her to say that she was his sister. According to Oriental custom this was true. She was the daughter of his father, but not of his mother and he had married her. But the story was meant to deceive and, as he feared, Sarai was taken into Pharaoh's harem. But God in His mercy intervened. Sarai was released unharmed and the party left Egypt, perhaps sadder and wiser by the experience. God's Word says, "The fear of man bringeth a snare." Peter learned that lesson the hard way as he sat and warmed himself at the world's fire. The man who boasted that he would go to prison and to death for the Lord's sake, when he was tested, denied the Lord. None of us should boast or say what we would do in the face of suffering, torture and death for Christ's sake. We are told not to fear them that kill the body, but to fear Him who is able to cast both soul and body into hell, Matthew 10:28.

On leaving Egypt and on the way back to the land of promise, Abram had a fourth test of his faith, that of FRICTION. There was a strife between the herdsmen of Abram's cattle and the herdsmen of Lot's cattle. The Canaanite and the Perizzite dwelled then in the land. The pagan population was looking on. Affluence has its dangers. The two men had to part. Abram graciously gave Lot the option of choosing which way to go. Sadly he made the wrong choice with devastating results. What he saw in Egypt influenced him in his choice. The well watered plains of Jordan were like the land of Egypt and he pitched his tent towards Sodom. That trip to Egypt had many long lasting repercussions.

The Scriptures and church history have many tragic examples of the results of friction among the people of God. One of Satan's chief weapons is the wedge. He will introduce the thin edge and then smash it home with his heavy sledge hammer. Abram and Lot, Paul and Barnabas are prime examples. The work of the Spirit is to build and to bind; the work of Satan is to divide and to destroy.

THE TWILIGHT OF FAITH

God had promised Abram that in him and in his seed all the families of the earth would be blessed. He said that his seed would be as the dust of the earth, Genesis 13:16, and as the stars of heaven. Abram believed God and it was counted to him for righteousness, Genesis 15:5,6. This was confirmed by a solemn covenant. There was to be an earthly seed and a heavenly one. His name was changed to Abraham, which means: "The father of many nations." But

Abraham had no child. The promise and everlasting covenant had been given by God, but many long years passed and there was no sign of its fulfilment. Had God forgotten? He is 85 years old and at his wife Sarah's suggestion he marries the Egyptian slave girl Hagar, and Ishmael is born. The result of that act and the lapse of faith has lasted for 40 centuries. The relations between Isaac and Ishmael, between Jew and Arab, are more acute today than ever before and will only be settled when the Son and seed of Abraham, the Messiah, returns and sets up His kingdom.

THE TRIUMPH OF FAITH

In due time Isaac, the seed and child of promise was born. God had not forgotten. But then the final test of Abraham's obedience and faith arrives: "Take now thy son, thine only son Isaac, whom thou lovest, and get thee into the land of Moriah; and offer him there for a burnt offering upon one of the mountains which I will tell thee of!" There was no hesitation on Abraham's part. Faith had now come to a peak. The writer to the Hebrews tells us that he "accounted that God was able to raise him (Isaac) up, even from the dead; from whence also he received him in a figure" Hebrews 11:19.

Many great Biblical words occur in Genesis 22 for the first time. "Only-begotten son," "love," "worship," "burnt offering," are examples. The chapter is a magnificent type of the substitutionary death of the Saviour. It is shown to be a transaction between a father and a son. In verse 17, the original covenant with Abraham is repeated and emphasised and a third metaphor of the seed is added. As well as the dust of the earth and the stars of heaven, the seed will be as the sand of the seashore. At the end of the chapter the genealogy of the bride of Isaac, Rebekah, is added.

Three times in Scripture Abraham is called "El Kalil" The Friend of God, 2 Chronicles 20:7; Isaiah 41:8; James 2:23. Four times in the New Testament we find the words: "Abraham believed God," Romans 4:3,17; Galatians 3:6; James 2:23. This was the keynote of his life.

When God calls and sends a man or woman into His work, He expects implicit obedience and simple faith in His promises to supply daily needs. Abraham is the outstanding example. In modern times George Muller of Bristol and Hudson Taylor of China taught us the lesson that the God of Abraham is the same today. Hudson Taylor said: "God's work, done in God's way, will always have God's support." The servant who has been sent by God, and who has been commended by, and has the confidence of his brethren in the local church, and who does a full day's work, will usually be supported. He may be tested like Abraham, but God is faithful and "utterly dependable" Hebrews 11:11 (Phillips Translation).

The Call of MOSES

Moses was one of the greatest men who ever lived. He had a profound influence on his contemporaries and a tremendous impact on history. His activities occupy 137 chapters of the Bible. He is the author of the Pentateuch and of Psalms 90,91. He is mentioned 80 times in the New Testament, more often than any other Old Testament character. He is called a Prophet, Deuteronomy 18:15; a Priest, Psalm 99:6; and a King in Jeshurun, Deuteronomy 33:5. Abraham is called the Friend of God; and Moses the Man of God, Psalm 90 title. If Abraham is the father of his country, demonstrating the principle of faith, Moses is the deliverer of his people from slavery, symbolizing the principle of leadership.

Moses had a divinely budgeted life: He lived 120 years.
1. Forty years in Egypt, learning to be somebody. The world's school.
2. Forty years in the desert, learning to be nobody. God's school.
3. Forty years as leader of the people of God, learning God's faithfulness.
Thus two-thirds of his life was preparation for his life's work.

(1) His Forty Years in Egypt

There were two profound influences in his early life. Pharaoh's daughter trained him for a royal position in Egypt, but his mother Jochabed prepared him for a place among the people of God. In Acts 7:23 Stephen tells us that he was learned in all the wisdom of the Egyptians and that

9   129

he was mighty in word and in deed. Thus three areas of his personality were developed. It is possible that he was a student at the "Temple of the Sun" called "the Oxford of ancient Egypt." He would learn to read and write hieroglyphics, to study maths, chemistry, and astronomy in which the Egyptians were experts. He would have a political, classical and royal education, and be familiar with court etiquette. He was in line for an important position in the world's greatest empire of the time. As well as this he "was mighty in word." He was a speaker and orator. Later he said that he couldn't speak, but that was after forty years at the backside of the desert speaking a different language. Then he was "mighty in deed." A practical man of action. Surely with all these qualifications, he was ready for his life's work! God did not think so. He had not learned meekness and self-control in man's school. He was too hasty. Seeing an Egyptian oppress a fellow Israelite, his temper flared, he killed the Egyptian and hid his body in the sand. Hebrews 11:24-26 tells us the other side of the story. In a magnificent passage four verbs are used: "By faith Moses REFUSED to be called the son of Pharaoh's daughter; CHOOSING rather to suffer affliction with the people of God...ESTEEMING the reproach of Christ greater riches than the treasures in Egypt: for he HAD RESPECT unto the recompense of the reward." The verb tenses point to a crisis. The first two are aorists, a point in time, the last two indicate the result. He fled to the desert and entered upon the second phase of his life, the backside of the desert.

(2) Forty Years at the Backside of the Desert
God's School

Elijah, John the Baptist and Paul had a desert experience. At the beginning of His public ministry, our Lord spent forty days in the desert and also at other times in His life, Mark 6:31. Was this wasted time? The desert is the place of testing and teaching. This is God's school where He trains His servants. Moses became a shepherd and a father, a valuable two-fold discipline. No one is fitted to counsel on family life until they have been in the school of suffering with God. Practical experience is a hard but valuable teacher.

While tending the flock, Moses saw a bush burning with fire and yet was not consumed. The time had come for his call to his life's work. The burning bush was the first of a series of sign miracles in which God dealt with five parts of his anatomy:

(a) His Feet. As Moses approached the burning bush to see the amazing sight, God spoke: Moses, Moses . . . Put off thy shoes from off thy feet, for the place whereon thou standest is holy ground. His first lesson was reverence in the presence of God. This was to be a primary trait in Moses' life. In our modern life, reverence for God is rapidly deteriorating. In addressing God in prayer and worship, and speaking about Him in ministry and evangelism we would appeal for reverence. The familiar language of the street or the telling of jokes to provoke a laugh, should find no place in the ministry of the man who has been in the presence of the Almighty Sovereign of the Universe.

(b) His Hand. "And the Lord said unto him, What is that in thine hand? And he said, A rod. And he said, cast it on the ground, and it became a serpent; and Moses fled from before it. And the Lord said unto Moses, Put forth thy hand and take it by the tail. And he put forth his hand and caught it, and it became a rod in his hand." The lesson is obvious. The rod was the shepherd's rod with which he tended the sheep. Later in Scripture it was to become the sceptre and a rod of iron, Psalm 2:9; Revelation 2:27. It is the symbol of authority and rule. In man's hand it is delegated authority. Moses was to use it five times in his subsequent life. The first man to have the rod of dominion or authority was Adam. In his case it was cast to the ground and became a deadly serpent. But another Man, the Last Adam has crushed the serpent's head. Moses the servant boldly takes it by the tail and it becomes again a rod in his hand. With it he faced Pharaoh, opened the Red Sea, smote the rock to bring out the living water and confronted Amalek, the enemy of the people, Exodus 17:9. Our Lord in the Great Commission said: All authority in heaven and in earth has been committed unto Me; go ye therefore ... Blessed is the man who has the ordination of the pierced hands and who carries the rod of delegated authority of the Risen and Glorified Christ in his hand.

(c) His Bosom. "And the Lord said furthermore unto him, Put now thy hand into thy bosom. And he put his hand into his bosom; and when he took it out, behold his hand was leprous as snow. And He said again, Put thy hand into thy bosom again. And he put his hand into his bosom again; and plucked it out of his bosom, and behold, it was turned again as his other flesh." Here is the lesson of the seat of human depravity and corruption. Paul said: "In me, that is in my flesh there dwelleth no good thing." The servant that goes forth into the work of the Lord and who has never learned this lesson, is of all men to be pitied. The old man and the flesh, the old habits and desires, and the depraved sinful nature are still with us. We are exhorted to put off the old man and his deeds, and to crucify or put to death the flesh. But they are with us as long as life shall last and there is plenty of tinder in our bosom on which Satan can cast his fiery darts and set it alight. But thank God for the indwelling Spirit of Life in Christ Jesus, and the Word of God and the Intercessor at God's right hand to give us the victory in time of need. The world outside, the flesh inside, and the devil beneath us have not changed. But we can be overcomers through Christ Jesus our Lord.

(d) His Mouth. "And Moses said unto the Lord, O my Lord, I am not eloquent, neither heretofore, nor since thou hast spoken unto thy servant, but I am slow of speech, and of a slow tongue. And the Lord said unto him, Who hath made man's mouth? ... Have not I the Lord?"

Moses' words are just an excuse. He did not want to go back to Egypt and face Pharaoh. In Egypt he was too hasty, now he is too hesitant. Most preachers at the beginning of their career feel the same way. Very few are eloquent or facile speakers. Usually it means hard work and careful study and only develops through time and experience. Mere volubility and talkativeness is a frightening gift. An endless talker who must have the floor at all times is a terrible bore and affliction. But what a comfort it is when

God says: "Now therefore go, and I will be with thy mouth, and teach thee what thou shalt say!" And what a joy it is when one feels that the Holy Spirit is speaking, unquenched and ungrieved, and God's people are being blessed and refreshed by the spoken word. The Apostle James has a lot to say about the tongue, both good and bad.

(e) **His Face**, Exodus 34:29-35. "The skin of Moses' face shone." Moses paid two forty day visits to the mountain top at Sinai. After the tragic episode of the worship of the golden calf and the smashing of the first tables of the law, he again ascends the mountain where he receives a new vision of the glory of God, a new commission and a renewed covenant. After a forty days fast, he comes down from the mountain with a transfigured face. He put a veil on his face while he talked with the people. Communion with God made his face shine. Paul applies this lesson in 2 Corinthians 3:13-16. Moses' experience was a transient fading glory, but under grace it is an increasing permanent glory. Communion with Christ in His Word under the operation of the Holy Spirit will produce the radiant countenance.

After these experiences, commencing with God's call, Moses is now ready to embark on his life's work of leadership with the people of God, to conduct them to the land of the promised inheritance.

(3) Forty Years as Leader in the Wilderness

The call of Moses at the burning bush and God's promise to be with him was the basis and foundation of the last forty years of his life. His confrontation with Pharaoh, the Passover and the Exodus, the covenant and the receiving of the ceremonial and the moral law at Sinai, the building of the Tabernacle, the overshadowing Shekinah, and God's presence and guidance during the forty years of wilderness wanderings, all had their stimulus and power from the fact that God had called and sent and fitted him to do the work.

The great need in the church today is competent leaders, sent and trained by God. We do not discount secular education, such as Moses had in Egypt; God can use that when it is dedicated to His service. But we must never bypass God's school at the backside of the desert. It is the prerogative of the Holy Spirit to raise up the men who will be leaders among His people. Human effort is vain, but God is able!

The Call of ELISHA

The period of Elijah and Elisha is the dark age of the monarchy in Israel. It is 58 years since the kingdom was divided under Jeroboam. In this brief period Judah had five reforming kings. Israel with its central government in Samaria had seven kings, all evil men. It was climaxed by King Ahab and his wicked consort, Jezebel. Ahab was a weak man, dominated by the worst woman in Israel's history. She introduced religious prostitution and political persecution. Baal and Ashtaroth were male and female deities, mixing religion with base and corrupt immorality. In Judah God used the king for reform and revival; but in Israel He used the prophet. Elijah and Elisha were two entirely different personalities. Elijah was a highlander from the mountains. To the polished courtiers of Samaria he was the wild man from Gilead, a shaggy lion of a man. His ministry was characterized by fire and water and denunciation. In contrast, the ministry of Elisha his successor was characterized by meal, oil and salt, the ingredients of the meal offering. The two men typify the life and ministry of John the Baptist, the Elijah of the New Testament; and Elisha the gentle fragrant ministry of the Lord Jesus.

Elisha's name means "God is Salvation." He was the son of Shaphat and lived at Abel-meholah, at the north end of the Jordan valley, and a little south of the Sea of Galilee. Twenty-nine times he is called a "man of God" and once a "holy man of God." He served the Lord 66 years, from his call, 1 Kings 19:19-21, till his death, 2 Kings 13:20, ten years with Elijah as an apprentice and 56 years alone. This is longer than any other Old Testament prophet.

His life is in four parts:

1. His call and preparation, 1 Kings 19.
2. His commission at Elijah's translation, 2 Kings 2.
3. The carrying out of his prophetic ministry, 2 Kings 3,4.
4. His wider ministry in a national sphere, 2 Kings 5-9.

His career extended over the reigns of Jehoram, Jehu, Jehoahaz, and Joash. He had the responsibility of carrying out the orders which Elijah had received at Horeb. His long steady life showed that he had learned the lesson which Elijah had heard on the mountain top, the voice of God is not in the fire or the tempest, but the still small voice heard in the secret of God's presence.

THE CALL OF ELISHA

God in His sovereignty had His eye on Elisha, 1 Kings 19:16. Elijah is simply following the instructions which he received at Horeb when he put his mantle upon Elisha as his successor. Elijah found him at his daily toil, ploughing with a yoke of oxen. God calls men from a wide variety of secular occupations. A wealthy city dweller, an heir to a throne, a shepherd, a fisherman and a tax collector. To earn one's living in an honourable trade or profession is a discipline which moulds a man's character. Those who step directly out of school into full-time service for the Lord without having this experience, lack one of the most valuable preparations for service in the work of the Lord. Paul was a tent maker and Peter a fisherman. To earn money the hard way and to spend it wisely is a valuable lesson in the school of life!

Three things resulted from the symbolic action of Elijah in putting his mantle on Elisha.

1. His request to kiss farewell to his father and mother. It shows a tender affectionate nature.
2. The sacrifice of his means of livelihood, killing the oxen and providing a feast for his friends. There was to be no turning back.
3. He followed and ministered to Elijah. For ten years he served with the older man in a menial capacity. "He

poured water on his hands" 2 Kings 3:11. It is likely to this passage that our Lord refers in Luke 9:61,62 "No man having put his hand to the plow and looking back is fit for the kingdom of God." Elisha made a complete break with the past.

HIS COMMISSION AND THE TASK AHEAD

There are many things about Elisha's call and career that remind us of Timothy and his relation to the Apostle Paul. The principle in Scripture seems to be, that the older man guides, counsels and instructs the younger man, and he in turn is willing to listen and learn and play a minor role until maturity comes.

A short time before Elijah's translation to heaven, he took Elisha on a last silent survey of the task ahead. They went together to Gilgal, Bethel, Jericho and Jordan. All these places had a blessed glorious past in the history of the nation, but now they are sunken into a condition of departure and apathy. Gilgal had been the base camp at the conquest of the land. It was here they carried out the rite of circumcision, they observed the passover and ate the old corn of the land. The Angel of the Lord had appeared in their midst and led by Joshua they faced and overthrew their enemies. But now Gilgal was one of the centres of national apostasy. Bethel—the House of God, had associations with Abraham and Jacob and the revealed presence of God. Now, one of Jeroboam's calves stood there, a centre of idolatry, and was called in contempt, Bethaven—the house of folly, Hosea 4:15. Jericho, the city of palm trees, had been devoted to destruction. In a display of divine power, the walls had fallen flat but Rahab with her scarlet cord in the window was saved. Now the city was a standing witness of defiance and rebellion. Heil the Bethelite had rebuilt Jericho, disregarding God's curse on the builder and consequently suffered in the death of his family. Jordan was the place where the ark rested and the waters stayed while the people passed over on resurrection ground. It once opened to let Israel into the land, now it opens to let Elijah out! On this circuit of the historical sites,

Elijah asked Elisha to remain at the various places. Was he trying to get rid of him? Surely not. It was a test to see how much he understood what was happening. Three times he said: "Tarry here!" It was a test of allegiance. But Elisha clave to him and "they two went on."

THE CRISIS, 2 Kings 2:8-14

When they crossed the Jordan, there were four striking episodes:
1. Elijah said unto Elisha: "Ask what I shall do for thee." And Elisha said: "I pray thee, let a double portion of thy spirit be upon me."
2. There was one condition. "If you see me as I am taken from thee, then it shall be so." Then appeared the chariot of fire and the horses of fire ... and Elijah went up in a whirlwind into heaven, and Elisha saw it!
3. The fallen mantle, the hairy garment of the prophet, the symbol of succession, of dedication and of power.
4. He cries: "My father, my father." He saw the one who had been his intimate guide and leader.

And so it is with the servant of Christ today. The measure of our likeness to Christ is dependent on our occupation with Christ ascended and glorified. The one condition is: "If you see me." The eye of faith sees Him at God's right hand. This new ministry flows from the experience of association with Christ in His death, resurrection and ascension.

Then Elisha lays aside his own clothes and takes up the fallen mantle!

THE NEW MINISTRY

From this point he goes back to the task of Reformation. He goes around the circuit of departure in reverse order. In Jericho there was bad water, in Bethel bad boys, in Gilgal bad food. When he crosses the Jordan his first difficulty is the skepticism of the sons of the prophets. They refused to believe in the translation of Elijah. For the bitter water of Jericho, his remedy is salt in a new cruse cast into the spring and the water was healed. At Gilgal there was poison in the pot which contained the food of the sons of the prophets. His antidote was wholesome meal, and there was no harm in the pot. At Jordan, Naaman the leper was told to dip himself seven times in the river and his leprosy was cleansed. But there was no remedy for Bethel where he was mocked, only judgment. For the poor bankrupt widow, his advice was to bring empty vessels and pour in the oil from her pathetic meagre supply. Salt, meal and oil, and the waters of Jordan were the ingredients which he used in his ministry of healing and comfort.

The outstanding lesson in the life of Elisha is DISCIPLESHIP. God's school for him was those ten years of humble service with Elijah. He poured water on his hands, but later God poured out the water of the Spirit upon him, and in turn, he poured it out on a needy thirsty world. The relationship between Moses and Joshua, Samuel and David, Jeremiah and Baruch, Paul and Timothy, demonstrates the principle. No man is fit to lead unless he is willing to be led and learn true humility, often in an obscure and menial situation. The old saying is so true: "It takes more grace than I can tell, to play the second fiddle well!"

The Call of ISAIAH

The discovery of the Dead Sea scrolls in 1947 was an outstanding event in archaeology. W.F. Albright calls it: "The greatest manuscript discovery of modern times." Among them were two copies of the prophecy of Isaiah, one of them complete and written in the old Hebrew script. The second one contains about one third of the text. They were copied at least 100 BC and are amazingly similar to the text we have in our Bibles today. This discovery has created renewed interest in the study of this beautiful prophetic book. The scrolls are preserved in a unique building in the centre of Jerusalem called "The Shrine of the Book."

Isaiah's life and ministry covers approximately 70 years, 750 BC-680 BC. He was contemporary with five kings of Judah: Uzziah, Jotham, Ahaz, Hezekiah and Manasseh. Some of these were good and some were bad men. Manasseh especially was a wicked man. It was the era approaching the Babylonian captivity, 586 BC. He was the son of Amos (not to be confused with the prophet Amos) and according to tradition was linked with the royal house of Judah. His book has been called a miniature Bible. The Bible has 66 books with 39 books in the Old Testament and 27 books in the New Testament. Isaiah has 66 chapters divided into two parts; 39 chapters paralleling Old Testament teaching, and 27 chapters paralleling New Testament doctrine. This second part commences with the prophetic ministry of John the Baptist, and ends with the New Heavens and the New Earth. In the centre is chapter 53 describing in prophetic detail the Messiah's birth, rejection, death, burial, and resurrection glory. The subject of the second part is "The Servant of Jehovah." In the most beautiful language of all literature, the coming Messiah is described in His humiliation and His coming glorious kingdom.

ISAIAH'S CALL

His call took place in the year that king Uzziah died. He was the king who, according to 2 Chronicles 26:20, was smitten with leprosy because he presumed to go into the temple to offer incense. This was the sin of pride and presumption. It was the sin of Nadab and Abihu, Leviticus 10:1-3. Uzziah had reigned 52 years and was the strongest, most capable king of Judah. He was a great soldier, statesman, agriculturalist and inventor. Science and strategy gave stability to his throne, but sin emptied it. Under the shock of this disaster, some seven years later, when the leper king died, the young Isaiah is brought into the presence of God and sees this vision of God's holiness and majesty.

The vision of chapter 6 is in three parts:
1. The vision of the Throne, vs.1-4.
2. The procedure at the Altar, vs.6-8.
3. The Challenge and the Commission, vs.9-13.

1. THE THRONE, vs.1-4

Isaiah is transferred in spirit from a scene of leprosy and defilement to one of unsullied holiness.

There are five things associated with the Throne:
1. **The Lord, Adonay.** A comparison of John 12:41 and Acts 28:25 shows that it was the Triune God.
2. **The Throne,** high and lifted up. Compare Isaiah 52:13; Philippians 2:9; Ephesians 1:21.
3. **The Temple.** The temple was the scene of Uzziah's sin, here of God's holiness and glory.
4. **The Seraphim,** the guardians of the throne. They have four wings for reverence and worship and two for service. They cry: "Holy, holy, holy, is the Lord of Hosts: the whole earth is full of His glory."

5. **The house was filled with smoke.** Perhaps the
Shekinah cloud, 2 Chronicles 5:13; Ezekiel 10:4.
Righteousness and judgment are the habitation of His
Throne, Psalm 97:2.

2. THE ALTAR, vs.6-8

As a result of this awesome vision of the Throne and of
God's holiness, Isaiah cries: "Woe is me!" He has used the
expression six times in the previous five chapters on other
people. The first woe is directed at the greedy merchants
who monopolized houses and real estate for themselves.
The second woe is against the drunkard and the pleasure
seeker. The third is uttered against those who sin wilfully
in defiance of God. The fourth against those who confuse
right and wrong. The last two are upon those who follow
their teachings. Isaiah uses strong language in condemning
these sinners. But in the light of the Throne and in the
presence of God he says: "Woe is me! for I am undone;
because I am a man of unclean lips; for mine eyes have seen
the King, the Lord of Hosts." He turns the sword in on
himself. "I am a leper in the midst of lepers," he cries.
Moses, Job, David, Peter and Paul, all had this experience. It
is a must for every servant whom God calls to do His work.

Then flew one of the seraphim, and taking a live coal
with the tongs from off the altar, laid it upon his mouth and
said: "Lò, this hath touched thy lips; and thine iniquity is
taken away and thy sin purged." The altar is not the golden
altar of incense, but the brazen altar of sacrifice where the
blood was shed. The altar is the answer to the Throne.

3. THE CHALLENGE AND THE COMMISSION, vs.9-13

After the conviction, confession, and the cleansing,
comes the Call "Whom shall I send and who will go for us."
Note the singular "I" and the plural "Us." It is the Triune
God who issues the call. Only those who have had the
experience of Isaiah can respond: "Here am I, send me."
First there is the Vision, then the Voice, and here the
Volunteer. Now Isaiah is ready for his commission. He was

given a most difficult task to perform. And He said: "Go, and tell this people, Hear ye indeed, but understand not; and see ye indeed, but perceive not. Make the heart of this people fat, and make their ears heavy, and shut their eyes, lest they see with their eyes and hear with their ears, and understand with their heart, and convert, and be healed." It was judicial hardening, deafening and blinding ministry. It affected his hearers' heart, ears, eyes and feet. In verse 10 it is heart, ears and eyes. From the heart, corruption flows to the ears and eyes. But from the ears and eyes, healing reaches the heart, Romans 10:17. This great dispensational passage was first fulfilled in dreadful reality on Israel and Judah at the Babylonian exile. This captivity had been predicted centuries before by Moses, Deuteronomy 30:18-20; 31:13. The passage is quoted seven times in the New Testament, and especially at three great crises; in Matthew 13 and John 12:40,41 at the rejection of Christ by Israel, and by Paul in Acts 28:25-27 at the end of his recorded public ministry when he turned from the Jews to the Gentile world, and finally in the great dispensational discussion in Romans 9 to 11.

When Isaiah asked how long he was to preach this message of judicial hardening to the nation, he was told: "Until the cities be wasted without inhabitant, and the houses without man, and the land be utterly desolate. And the Lord have removed men far away; and there be a great forsaking in the midst of the land." In other words he was to preach until there was nobody left to whom to preach! What a discouraging mission to a brilliant man like Isaiah who had such ability and a glorious message. It reminds us of many honoured servants of God in Moslem lands who spend their lives in dedicated service with little or no visible results. The Gospel is like the heat of the sun, it melts the wax but hardens the clay, 2 Corinthians 2:15.

But the commission ends with a message of hope. A covenant keeping God could never allow the message to end in defeat. A tithe or remnant would return from the captivity. The life germ in the rooted stump of the tree would survive. In it would be the Holy Seed. The messianic Holy Seed, the seed of the woman secures the perpetuity of the nation. One thing that kept Israel from being wiped out completely was the necessity of preserving the line of descent of the Messiah.

Isaiah's mission and message from this point till his death was twofold: The warning of judgment on the apostate nation, and the glorious message of hope; the Person, the coming, and the mission of the Messiah.

The whole of the book of Isaiah contains traces of the lasting impression made upon Isaiah by the vision of the holiness of God which he received at his call in chapter 6. While his main theme is the Messianic hope, yet in every part of the book he stresses the necessity of a holy life in keeping with the holiness of God. The title, "The Holy One of Israel" occurs 25 times, twelve times in the first part, and thirteen times in the second part, showing the unity of the book. It is found only six times in all the rest of the Old Testament. Tradition says that Isaiah was martyred by being placed inside a hollow tree and the tree sawn in two. (cf. Hebrews 11:37). Whether the tradition is authentic or not, the critics have tried to do the same with his book. But this great title of God and its underlying theme shows that the book is a unit and completely authoritative for the servant of God today.

The Call of SIMON PETER

The Apostle Peter, whose original name was Simon, was the son of Jonas or John. He was a fisherman, an inhabitant of Bethsaida, but subsequently lived with his family at Capernaum. He was married. He was a born leader and inveterate talker. He had a transparent enthusiastic disposition. He is always mentioned first in the list of the apostles. He was bold, confident, frank, but impulsive. He was inquisitive and asked more questions then anyone else in the New Testament. He was emotional and affectionate, a great elemental human being. Henry Drummond said about Moody that "He was the greatest human being he ever knew." Not clever or intellectual, but HUMAN!

In considering Peter's life as recorded in the Scriptures, there are four times that God called him:

1. The Call to Salvation, John 1:35-42.
2. The Call to be a Fisher of Men, Mark 1:16-20; Luke 5:1-11.
3. The Call to Apostleship, Matthew 10:1-5.
4. The Call to be a Shepherd, John 21.

1. THE CALL TO SALVATION, John 1:35-42.

After the introductory prologue, vs.1-18, in John's Gospel, four great dispensational days are outlined in chapter 1.

1. The day of the Baptist's witness to Christ, vs.19-28.
2. The day of witness to the Cross and the descending Spirit, vs.29-34.
3. The day of gathering to Christ, vs.35-42.
4. The day of the opened heaven, vs.43-51.

It was during this third day that Peter was brought to Christ by his brother Andrew. Andrew had found the Messiah and immediately went after his brother and brought him to Jesus. And when Jesus beheld him, looked through him with a searching penetrating look, He said: "Thou art Simon the son of Jonas: thou shalt be called Cephas, which is by interpretation, a stone." The amazing thing here is that Peter didn't utter a word. He was struck dumb with astonishment. The changed name shows that the Lord can see us as we are and visualize what we can become. But many years lie between. Sometimes Peter looked like sand. Geologists tell us that rock is the result of fire, pressure and time. The result of that day's interview: the Lord was first just a Rabbi, but now He is Messiah, the Christ.

2. THE CALL TO BE A FISHER OF MEN
Mark 1:16-20; Luke 5:1-11

Some expositors regard Luke 5 as a fuller account of the incident recorded in Mark 1. It takes place about a year after Peter first met the Lord at Jordan. There was a fishing partnership, consisting of Peter and Andrew, James and John and their father Zebedee. Apparently Simon Peter was the head of the company, Luke 5:20. Business was flourishing, as they had hired servants, Mark 1:20. A comparison of three parallel passages in the Gospels shows that there were four operations with the fishing nets: (1) Washing the nets, Luke 5:2. (2) Letting down the net, Luke 5:4. (3) Casting the net, (a small one), Mark 1:16. (4) Mending the nets, Mark 1:19.

As Jesus was preaching the Word of God on the shore of the Sea of Galilee and as the crowd pressed on Him, He borrowed Peter's boat and using it as a pulpit, pushing out a little from the shore, He addressed the multitude. When He had finished speaking, He asked Peter to go out to deep water and lower the net. But Peter answered: "Master, we have toiled all night and have taken nothing; nevertheless at thy word I will let down the net. And when they had this done, they enclosed a great multitude of fishes; and their net brake. When Simon Peter saw it, he fell down at Jesus' knees, saying: Depart from me for I am a sinful man, O Lord. And Jesus said: Fear not, from henceforth thou shalt catch men. And when they had brought their ships to land, they forsook all and followed Him."

The lesson for the evangelist is obvious. At Pentecost Peter let down the net of the Gospel and 3,000 were brought in and for all there were so many, yet was not the net broken. But as well as casting the net in the shallows and letting it down into the deep, the fisher of men must be careful to wash the net and keep it clean, and to keep it mended so that fish may not slip through the holes.

3. THE CALL TO BE AN APOSTLE
Matthew 10:1-5

After a whole night spent in prayer on the mountainside, Jesus chose twelve from among His disciples and called them apostles, Luke 6:12,13. The account in Mark 3:13,14 stresses His sovereign choice: "He goeth up into a mountain, and calleth unto Him whom He would; and they came unto Him. And He ordained twelve that they should be with Him, and that He might send them forth to preach." "That they should be with Him." A.T. Robertson calls this "a peripatetic theological school!" He also points out that Luke 6 makes it plain that they were chosen just before the Sermon on the Mount. In Matthew 10 they are named, but chosen in chapter 5. He keeps them by His side for about a year and then sends them forth two by two as missionaries.

There are some today who claim to be apostles. But the Scriptures make it clear that these were a unique company of men whose function later on was to lay the foundations of the Church. In the New Jerusalem in Revelation 21:14 we read: "And the wall of the city had twelve foundations, and in them the names of the twelve apostles of the Lamb." The qualifications of an apostle are outlined in Acts 1:21,22 when Matthias was chosen to take the place of Judas Iscariot, "Wherefore of these men which have companied with us all the time that the Lord Jesus went in and out among us, beginning from the baptism of John, unto that same day that He was taken up from us, must one be ordained to be a witness with us of His resurrection." Obviously there is no one today who has these qualifications. The apostleship of the Apostle Paul was unique. He too had seen the Lord in resurrection and had been commissioned by Him. But it is a dangerous thing today for anyone to make high claims and assume exalted titles.

Peter is always mentioned first among the apostles and was given the great privilege of opening the door of the kingdom to the Jew at Pentecost and to the Gentile at Caesarea, Acts 10.

4. THE CALL TO BE A SHEPHERD
John 21

John 21 is an inspired appendix to the Gospel by John and a preface to the Acts of the Apostles, linking the two together. There are two great lessons in the chapter. First a lesson in catching fish and then a lesson in feeding sheep. They illustrate the Church's twofold task in evangelism and pastoral care of God's people.

Impulsive and restless Peter says: "I go afishing" and six others say: "We also go with thee." They were representative men and among them experts in catching fish. But again they toiled all night and caught nothing. In the morning the Risen Lord stood on the shore and called: "Lads, have ye any fish?" They answered with a disgruntled monosyllable, "No!" He called again: "Cast the net on the right side and ye shall find. They cast therefore and now they were not able to draw it for the multitude of fishes."

The lesson is on the surface. Any work undertaken without the command and the presence of the Risen Lord is only a waste of time! We can have a group of experts who know all the theory of fishing, but if He is not there directing operations, it is completely futile. Another thing, Peter needed to be restored to the confidence of his brethren. He had denied the Lord publicly and he needed to be restored publicly.

The Lord had lit a little charcoal fire on the shore. It was the same type of a fire where Peter had denied the Lord in Pilate's judgment hall. Three times Peter had denied the Lord and three times the question is asked: "Simon, son of Jonas, lovest thou Me?" And three times Peter replies: "Lord thou knowest that I love Thee." Then he receives a threefold commission: "Feed my lambs." "Tend my sheep." "Feed my dear sheep" (the diminutive of affection). At the beginning of his experience with the Lord, he received the command: "Come after Me," Mark 1:17; here the command is repeated: "Keep on following Me," John 21:22.

So here Peter has been called and commissioned to be a fisher of men and a shepherd of sheep.

At the end of his first epistle, Peter passes on the torch to his brethren, who will have the responsibility after he has gone. "The elders which are among you I exhort, who am also an elder and a witness of the sufferings of Christ, and also a partaker of the glory that shall be revealed: Feed the flock of God which is among you, taking the oversight thereof, not by constraint, but willingly; not for filthy lucre, but of a ready mind; neither as being lords over God's heritage, but being ensamples to the flock. And when the chief Shepherd shall appear, ye shall receive a crown of glory that fadeth not away."

May the great Head of the Church, that Great Shepherd of the sheep, raise up many fishers of men and undershepherds to feed and tend and care for the flock today!

The Call of PAUL THE APOSTLE

The Apostle Paul is one of the greatest men of all time. Yet he himself did not think so. He calls himself less than the least of all saints. That he was a man chosen by God at a critical period in world history is beyond question. There were three events of world importance prior to Paul's birth. The career of Alexander the Great had spread the knowledge of the Greek language over the then known world. The rise of the Roman empire gave ease of communications and protection of law. The Jewish dispersion called the Diaspora with the Jewish belief in One God and their possession of the Old Testament Scriptures had penetrated into most of the strategic centres and cities. There was the necessity in the early church for a man who had all these things in his background. That man was Saul of Tarsus, later called Paul. He was a Hebrew by birth, a Roman citizen, and as well as the Greek language, spoke Hebrew, Aramaic and possibly a number of other languages.

A.T. Robertson conjectures he was born about AD 1 and died in AD 66. How much he accomplished in those 66 years! His intellect, courage, perseverance, sympathy, integrity and tact show that he was a man of rich personality.

His life could be divided into four periods:

1. SAUL THE PHARISEE

This period occupied about 35 years, approximately one half of his life. He was born in Tarsus, the Greek capital of Cilicia in southeast Asia Minor. He calls it no mean city.

Along with Athens and Alexandria it was one of three university cities. Its students linked East and West. He was a Benjamite with the same name as Israel's first king. He learned the trade of making goat's hair tents. He was brought up in a liberal Greek atmosphere, but was sent to Jerusalem for his theological education "at the feet of Gamaliel." He became a strict Pharisee characterized by intolerance and bigotry. It is an open question whether he was a member of the Sanhedrin, the Jewish parliament, or not. At the death of Stephen he says he cast his vote. He became a bitter persecutor and antagonist of the Christians. In later years, in two of his speeches and in four of his epistles he refers to those days of persecution. He was "the Benjamite ravening wolf."

2. HIS CONVERSION AND CALL TO SERVICE

At the peak of his persecuting career, Paul was arrested on the Damascus road. He saw the Risen Christ and heard His voice. His conversion was instantaneous and dramatic. He uses three words to describe it; he was apprehended, Philippians 3:12; illuminated, Acts 26:13; and it was a revelation, Galatians 1:16. He tells us that his conversion was a pattern or type of what will happen to the nation, 1 Timothy 1:16.

His Call to Service. This was fivefold:
1. Like Samson and John the Baptist, God chose him before he was born. "But when it pleased God, who separated me from my mother's womb, and called me by His grace," Galatians 1:15.
2. At his conversion. When he was arraigned before Agrippa, he describes the commission he received at his conversion: "Rise, stand upon thy feet, for I have appeared unto thee for this purpose, to make thee a minister and a witness, both of these things which thou hast seen, and of those in the which I will appear unto thee; delivering thee from the people, and from the Gentiles, unto whom now I send thee, Acts 26:15-18.
3. To Ananias of Damascus. "But the Lord said unto him,

Go thy way, for he is a chosen vessel unto Me, to bear My name before the Gentiles and kings, and the children of Israel," Acts 9:15.
4. In a trance in Jerusalem. Amidst the uproar of a lynching mob. "Depart, for I will send thee far hence to the Gentiles," Acts 22:17-21.
5. At Antioch. "The Holy Ghost said, Separate me Saul and Barnabas for the work whereunto I have called them," Acts 13:2.
NOTE: The Holy Trinity was involved in his call. It was God who called him before he was born, Galatians 1:15; it was the Lord at his conversion; and it was the Holy Ghost at Antioch.

His Preparation for Service. This lasted approximately 10 years. First at Damascus, Acts 9:20,21; then in Arabia, Galatians 1:17; in Damascus again, Acts 9:22-25; a visit to Jerusalem, Acts 9:26-30, Galatians 1:18; in his home city of Tarsus, Acts 9:30; 11:25; then in Antioch with Barnabas and the local church. This period of preparation was important. It gave him time for study and re-adjustment of his thinking. His friend Barnabas was a great help and encouragement at this time.

3. PAUL THE PIONEER AND CHURCH PLANTER

This period in Paul's life lasted about 15 years from AD 44-60. In three great missionary journeys, local churches were planted at strategic centres in all four provinces of the Roman empire. A writer in the Geographic magazine reckons that Paul travelled about 12,000 miles with the Gospel. On land it was mostly on foot. In those days there were no railways, cars, planes, luxurious passenger ships or hotels. From his first missionary journey to his death, he travelled on foot 5,580 miles and by sea 6,770 miles, a total of 12,350 miles. When we consider that he was a sick man, it is an amazing physical performance. It is rather remarkable too, that in the historical account in the Acts, finances are never mentioned. He often worked with his hands to provide the necessities of life and we know he received love gifts from the church at Philippi, but there was no appeal for funds!

4. PAUL THE PRISONER

In the last six years of Paul's life, there were three imprisonments. First in Caesarea, then two years of house arrest in Rome, and after a short period of liberty, his final imprisonment and execution. But like John Bunyan and Samuel Rutherford his time in confinement was not wasted. The eagle was chained but rendered service with eternal results. The Gospel reached right into Nero's household, his pen was busy and his written ministry has left us a precious heritage. The Prison Epistles of Ephesians, Philippians and Colossians and the lovely little letter to Philemon are treasures beyond all price. Then there are the Pastoral Epistles of 1 and 2 Timothy and Titus giving Paul's final instructions about personal and church life and order.

Paul's call, commission and career are a tremendous encouragement and pattern for us today. There is a great need everywhere for the Gospel pioneer and church planter, and for those who are gifted to use their pen for God's glory and for the edification of the saints.

Conclusion

We have considered six men, four in the Old Testament and two in the New Testament, who were called and sent and fitted by God to engage in service. All of them are described in considerable detail. They lived at different periods of history and most were different in their background and education.

Now it is time to enquire if there was something common to them all. What is the common denominator that inspired and sustained them in their work for God? Are the principles that governed them, relevant for the present day? These are important questions that demand an answer.

While we use the term "men" the same principles are applicable to women also. They have an important part to play in the sphere where God has placed them.

1. First and above all, God is sovereign in those He chooses to do His work. He loves to take unpromising material and mould and polish it according to His own sovereign will.
2. God speaks and reveals Himself to each one individually in the secret of His presence. The question may be asked: How does God speak to His children today and call them? Not in a vision or a voice as in the olden days, or a prophetic voice as in Acts 13. But He speaks in His Word. Today He uses His Word in the New Birth and also in the call to service.
3. Then God always prepares His instrument. Often this is a long process. With Moses it was 80 years; with John the Baptist 30 years; with Paul 10 years, and even our

154

Lord spent 30 years in the obscurity of Nazareth. The time of preparation is not wasted time.

4. Those who were called were vessels fitted for the work to be done. They were not square pegs in a round hole. They had the natural and spiritual qualifications for the task ahead.

5. They had a heavy burden and exercise about the need in their day and were men of prayer. Today we have the indwelling Spirit of God who creates that burden and who guides us step by step.

6. Their work had the seal of God's blessing upon it.

7. The call was always to a work and not just to a place or location. It is true that Abraham was called to go to a specific country but his work was to demonstrate the principle of faith in his life.

Again we would emphasize the principle of seeking the advice and counsel of godly spiritual men who know the Word. In a multitude of counsellors there is safety, Proverbs 11:14.

When these seven principles coincide in the life of any believer, we can be sure that God is speaking and has a work for the individual to perform.

May God raise up servants with the calibre of these men today!

"God had only one Son and He was a missionary."
David Livingstone

"Whom shall I send, and who will go for us?" Isa. 6:8